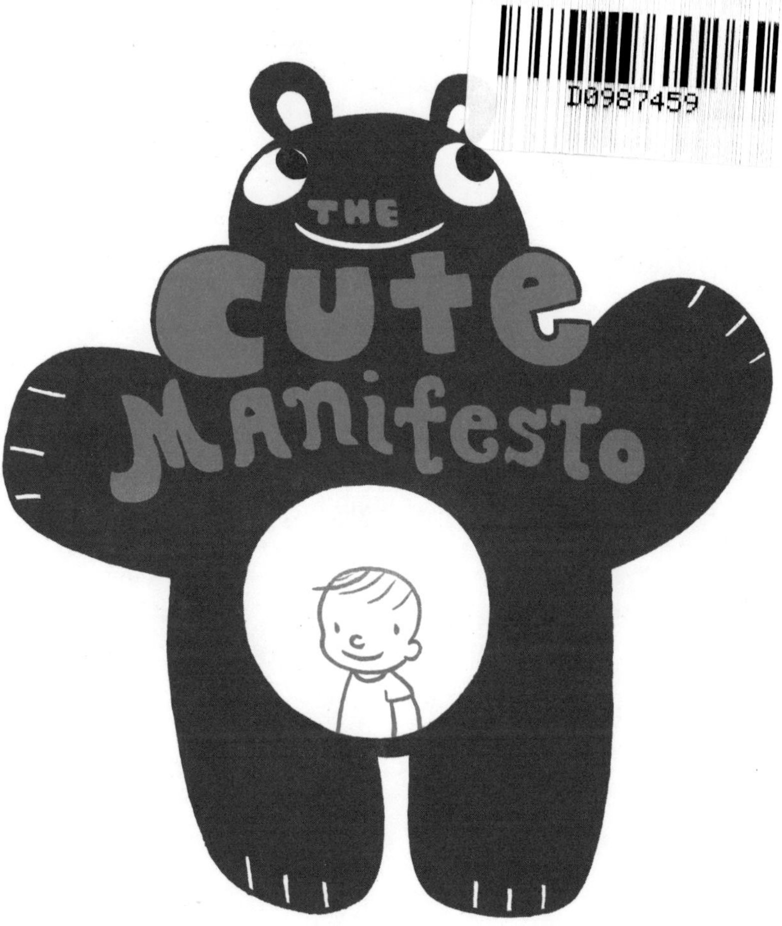
THE
Cute
Manifesto

The Cute Manifesto by James Kochalka

Alternative Comics
503 NW 37th Ave.
Gainesville, FL 32609-2204
352.373.6336
jmason@indyworld.com
www.indyworld.com/altcomics

Publisher: Jeff Mason.
Production Design: Tom Devlin and James Kochalka.

First printing, July 2005.
13-digit ISBN: 978-1-891867-73-6
10-digit ISBN: 1-891867-73-3
10 9 8 7 6 5 4 3 2 1

Printed in Canada.

# CONTENTS:

⭐ CRAFT IS THE ENEMY ⭐

⚡ CRAFT IS NOT A FRIEND ⚡

 SUNBURN

REINVENTING EVERYTHING
~ PART ONE ~

REINVENTING EVERYTHING
~ PART TWO ~

 THE CUTE MANIFESTO

*the horrible truth about comics*

AND THE LAST MINUTE
ADDITION:

SPELUNKING FOR
SLIPPERY CAVE FISH

CRAFT IS THE ENEMY

# CRAFT IS THE ENEMY

I'm not exactly sure why I am writing this letter, but I've been reading *The Comics Journal #188* for a couple hours now and my mind has just been racing and blood pounding. My excitement with the power and possibilities of comics mixed with the fear of a royally screwed-up marketplace...well, let's just say I've got a weird shaky adrenaline rush.

I just felt suddenly like I had to write and say craft is the enemy! You could labor your whole life perfecting your "craft," struggling to draw better, hoping one day to have the skills to produce a truly great comic...If this is how you are thinking you will never produce this great comic, this powerful work of art, that you dream of. There's nothing wrong in trying to draw well, but that is not of primary importance.

What every creator should do, must do, is use the skills they have right now. A great masterpiece is within reach if only your will power is strong enough (just like Green Lantern.) Just look within yourself and say what you have to say.

Cezanne and Jackson Pollock (and many other great painters) were horrible draftsmen! It was only through their sheer will to be great that they were great. The fire they had inside eclipsed their lack of technical skill. Although they started out shaky and even laughable, they went on to create staggering works of art.

This letter is not for the established creators...they're hopeless. This is for the young bucks and does...let's kick some fucking ass!

CRAFT IS NOT A FRIEND

# CRAFT IS NOT A FRIEND

Okay, I will say it again in a different way for the idiots who couldn't understand me the first time.

When you are shooting for immortality, anything less than a stunning achievement is a failure. Creating a powerful work of art is like running and leaping across a chasm. It takes all of your strength and you'll be dashed on the rocks and fall to your death. Being a craftsman is like sitting in your woodshop all day carefully building a chair and when you are done you sit on it. Are comics craft? Well, certainly any cartoonist you are likely to meet will tell you "yes." And that's a big problem. Craft is boring. Ever been to a crafts fair? Not unlike a comics convention. Craft sucks.

When a cartoonist sits down to draw, and their goal is to draw well, they are doomed to failure. No matter how much they practice the best they can hope for is to become a polished hack aping their preconceived ideal of "good comics," to become a mere hollow shell of the cartoonists who came before.

For one reason, there is no objective "good" in art. Someone could conceivably think *Spawn* is well drawn and think *Peanuts* is poorly drawn (although that sounds insane to me). So if you are trying to draw well what you are shooting for is illusory. There is, objectively, no such thing.

However, if you are burning up inside with the need to express yourself, if there's something you desperately need to say, when you sit down at the drawing table you think "how am I going to say this? How am I going to express myself so that people will understand?" The art will be slave to the content. Either the artist expresses the meaning, emotion, and power of their vision or they do not. The comic succeeds or fails on these terms. The notion of quality is meaningless.

# SUNBURN

HERE I AM,
ON THIS PLANET.

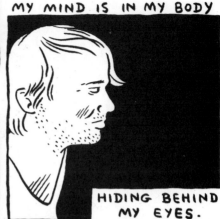

MY MIND IS IN MY BODY

HIDING BEHIND
MY EYES.

MY BODY IS TAKING A SHIT

AFTERWARDS, MY HANDS
WILL WASH THEMSELVES.

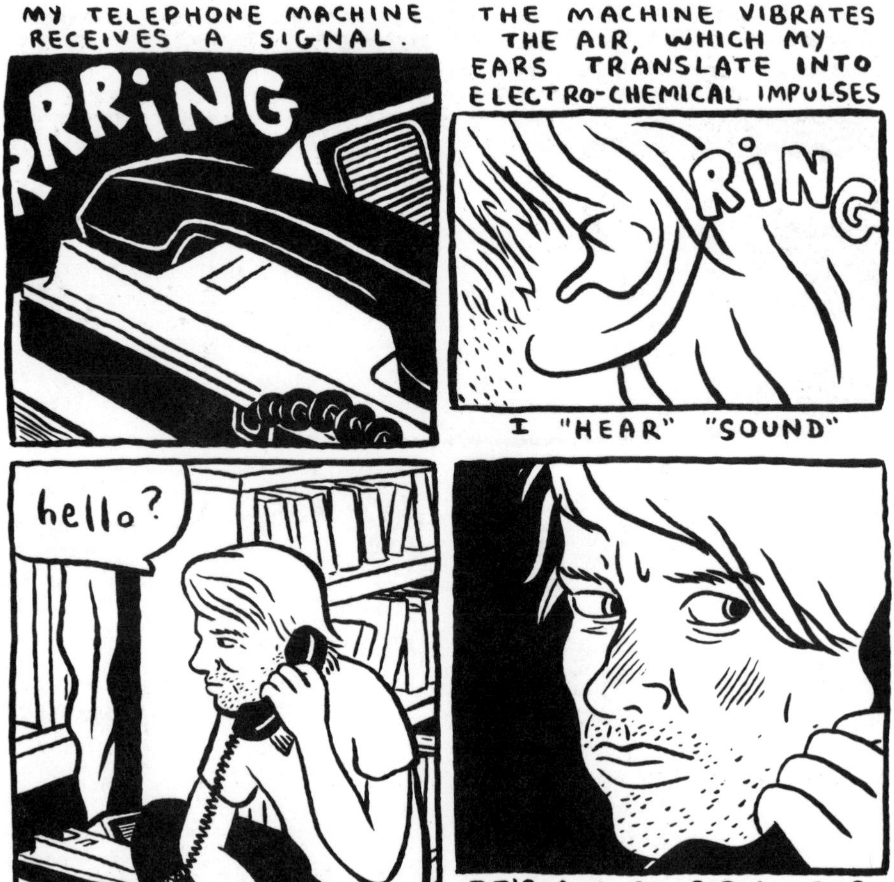
MY TELEPHONE MACHINE RECEIVES A SIGNAL.
RRRING
THE MACHINE VIBRATES THE AIR, WHICH MY EARS TRANSLATE INTO ELECTRO-CHEMICAL IMPULSES
RING
I "HEAR" "SOUND"
hello?
IT'S ALL SO RIDICULOUS.

FIVE BILLION PEOPLE ACROSS THE PLANET DESPERATELY SUCKING IN AIR AND BLOWING IT OUT THROUGH THEIR VOICE BOXES WHICH GURGLE AND VIBRATE IN A FEEBLE ATTEMPT TO COMMUNICATE

ah, NO
you have a WRONG Number
No, that's O.K.
good bye

OUTSIDE, RADIATION RAINS DOWN FROM THE SUN. PLANTS SOAK IT IN AND THEY GROW.

PEOPLE SOAK IT IN AND THEIR SKIN BURNS

YESTERDAY, MY SKIN WAS LIGHTLY BURNED IN THIS FASHION.

THE TINGLE REMINDS ME THAT MY BODY AND MIND ARE CONNECTED.

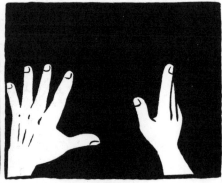

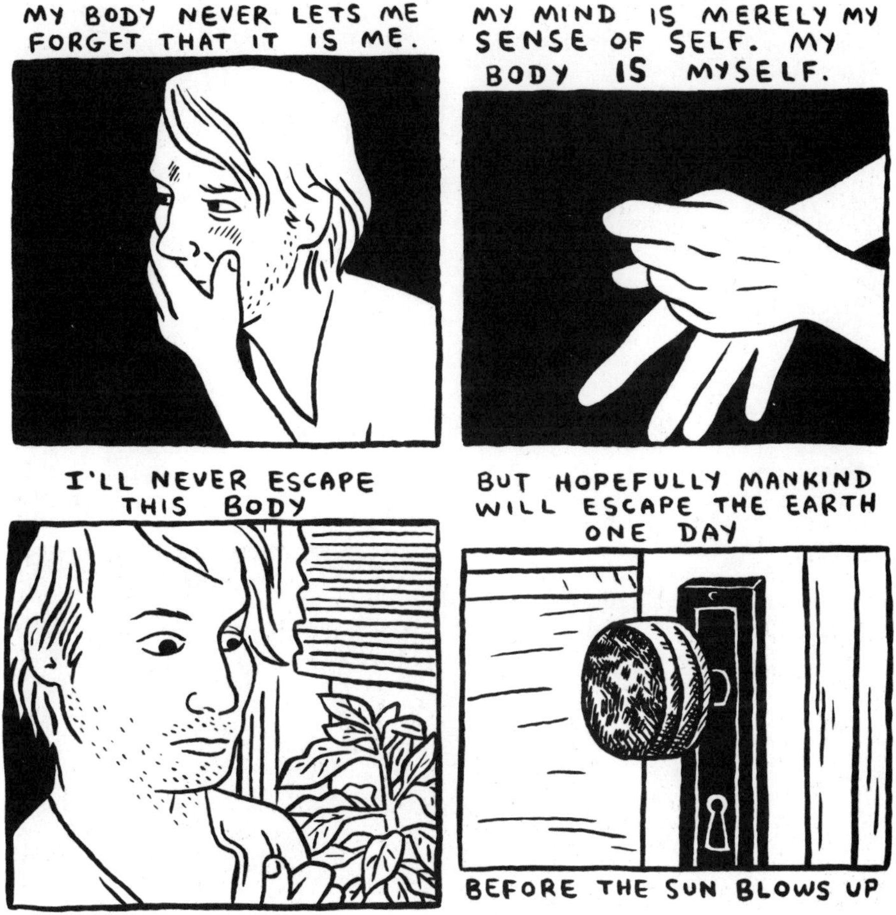
MY BODY NEVER LETS ME FORGET THAT IT IS ME.
MY MIND IS MERELY MY SENSE OF SELF. MY BODY IS MYSELF.
I'LL NEVER ESCAPE THIS BODY
BUT HOPEFULLY MANKIND WILL ESCAPE THE EARTH ONE DAY
BEFORE THE SUN BLOWS UP

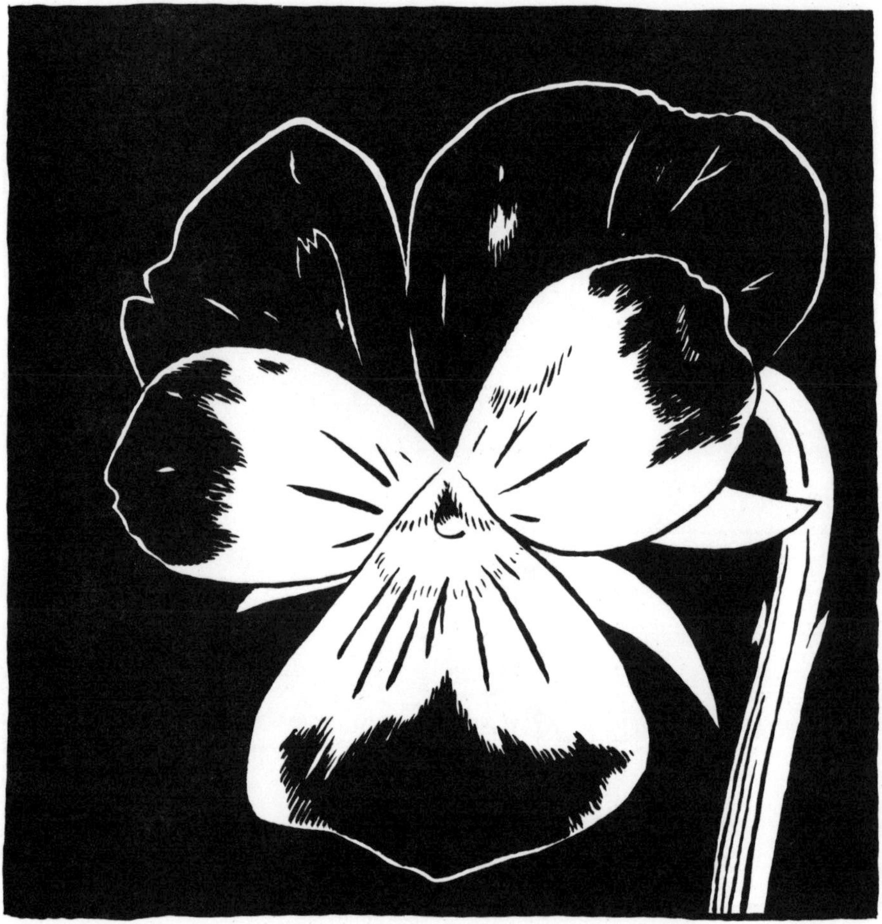

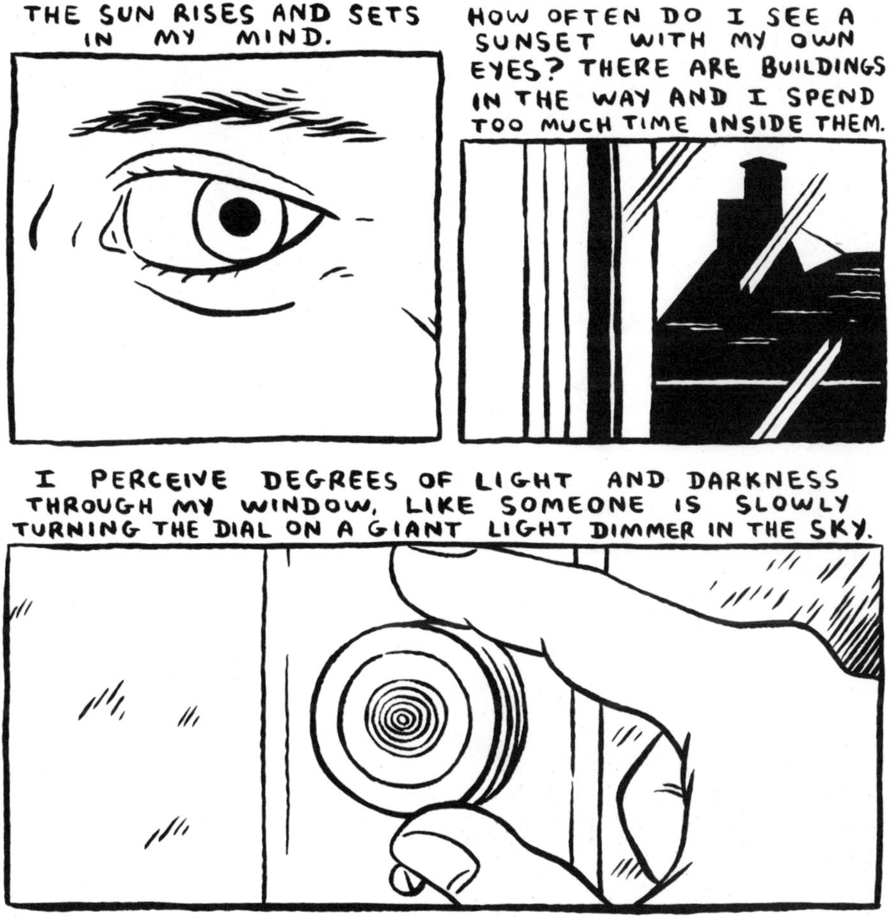
THE SUN RISES AND SETS IN MY MIND.
HOW OFTEN DO I SEE A SUNSET WITH MY OWN EYES? THERE ARE BUILDINGS IN THE WAY AND I SPEND TOO MUCH TIME INSIDE THEM.
I PERCEIVE DEGREES OF LIGHT AND DARKNESS THROUGH MY WINDOW, LIKE SOMEONE IS SLOWLY TURNING THE DIAL ON A GIANT LIGHT DIMMER IN THE SKY.

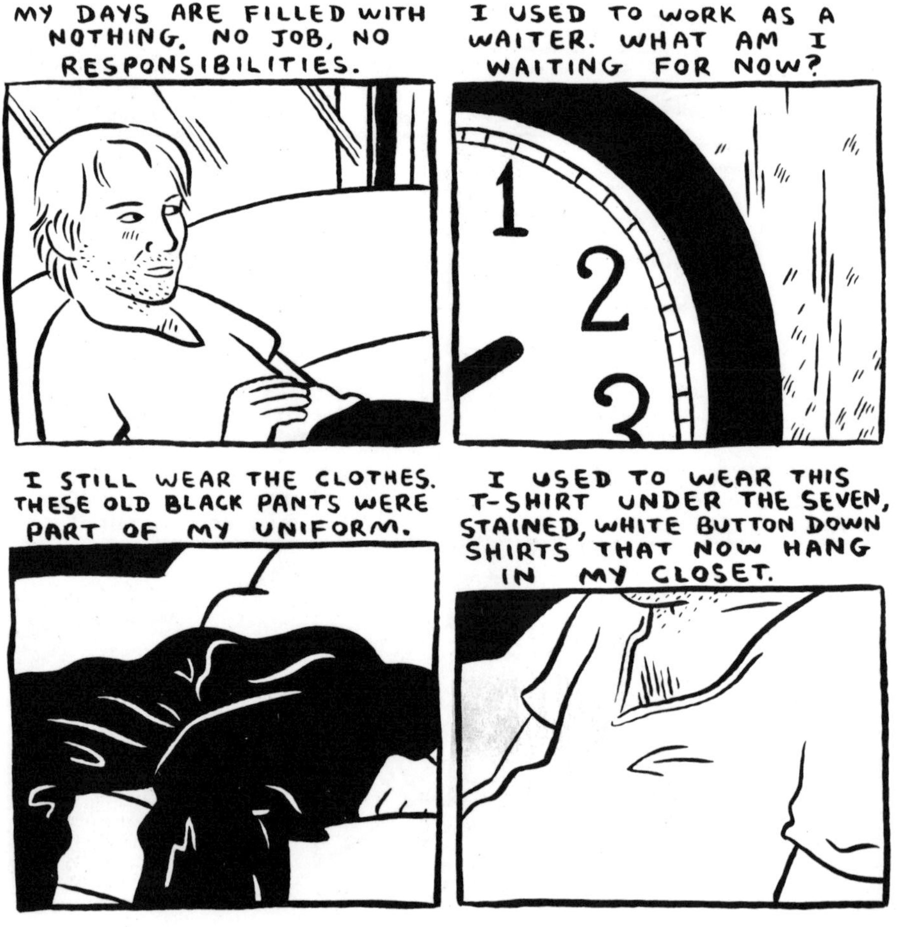
MY DAYS ARE FILLED WITH NOTHING. NO JOB, NO RESPONSIBILITIES.
I USED TO WORK AS A WAITER. WHAT AM I WAITING FOR NOW?
I STILL WEAR THE CLOTHES. THESE OLD BLACK PANTS WERE PART OF MY UNIFORM.
I USED TO WEAR THIS T-SHIRT UNDER THE SEVEN, STAINED, WHITE BUTTON DOWN SHIRTS THAT NOW HANG IN MY CLOSET.

IT MIGHT BE NICE TO GET SOME NEW CLOTHES, BUT SO WHAT? IT MIGHT BE NICE TO DO A LOT OF THINGS.

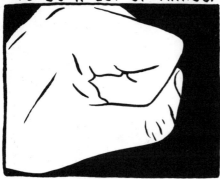

WHY DO I NEED NEW CLOTHES TO HANG ON MY BODY?

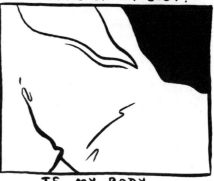

IS MY BODY A CLOTHES HANGER?

MY BODY IS A WEIRD MACHINE OF GRINDING BONE AND SPURTING BLOOD.

IT WILL CONTINUALLY GROW MY HAIR AND FINGERNAILS UNTIL EVENTUALLY IT BECOMES TOO OLD AND TIRED AND DIES.

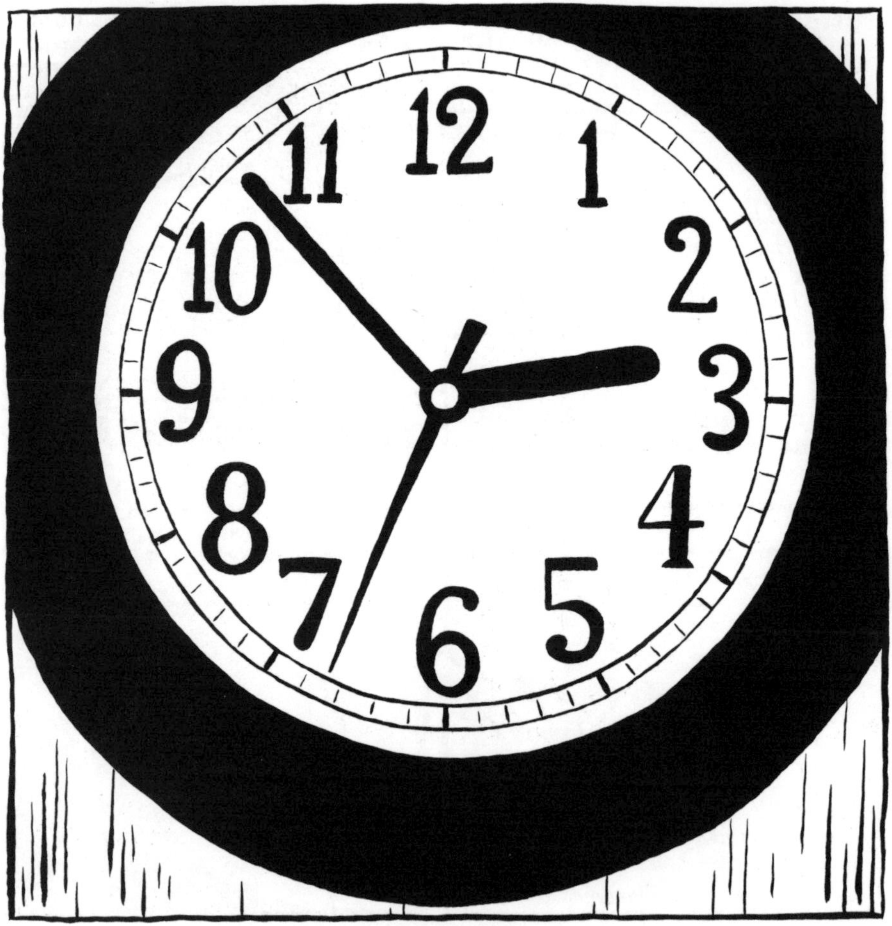
12
1
2
3
4
5
6
7
8
9
10
11

AND WHEN MY BODY DIES SO
WILL MY PRECIOUS MIND.
(MY HAIR IS ALREADY
STARTING TO FALL OUT.)

THE BLACK SILENCE WILL COME,
AND I WILL BE NOWHERE.

BUT WHERE AM I NOW?

BUT SOMETIMES I SENSE
MYSELF IN MY ELBOW
OR IN MY TOE

IT USUALLY FEELS LIKE I'M
HIDDEN SOMEWHERE BEHIND
MY EYES AND BETWEEN MY EARS.

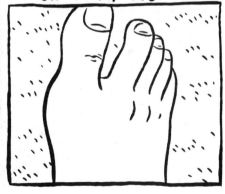

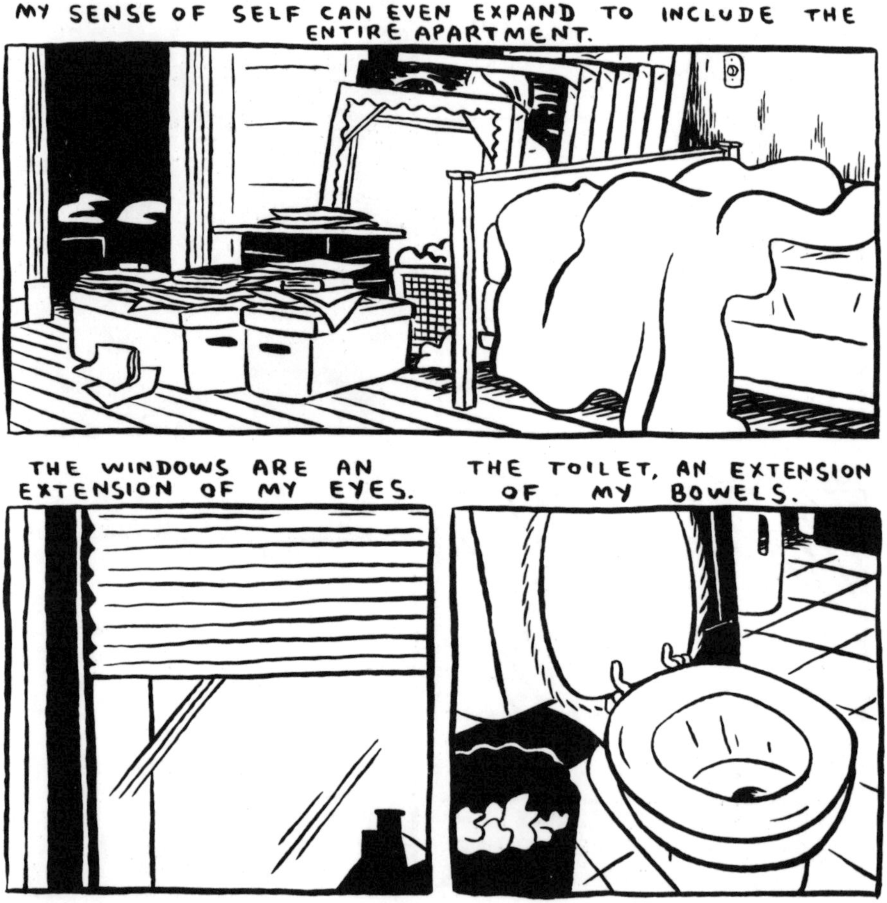
MY SENSE OF SELF CAN EVEN EXPAND TO INCLUDE THE ENTIRE APARTMENT.
THE WINDOWS ARE AN EXTENSION OF MY EYES.
THE TOILET, AN EXTENSION OF MY BOWELS.

CERTAINLY THIS APARTMENT HAS BECOME AS FAMILIAR
TO ME AS MY OWN BODY.

I'M COMFORTABLE.

I FIT NICELY HERE.

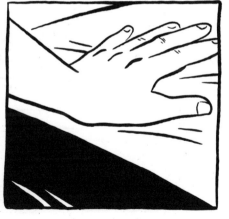

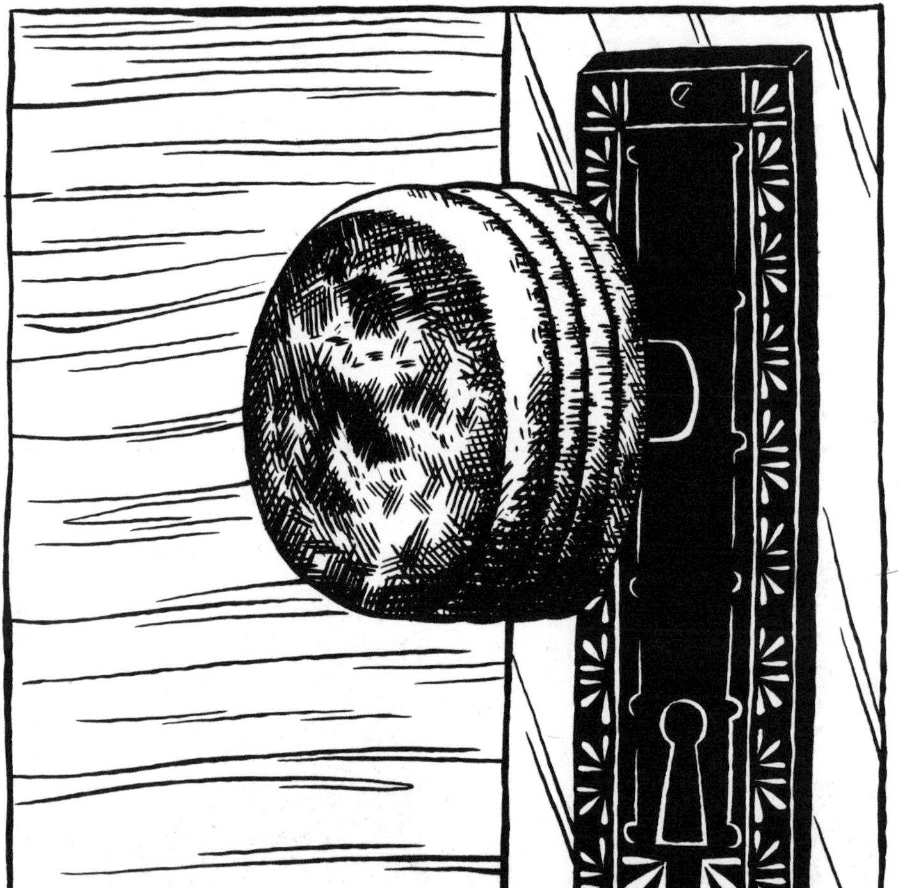

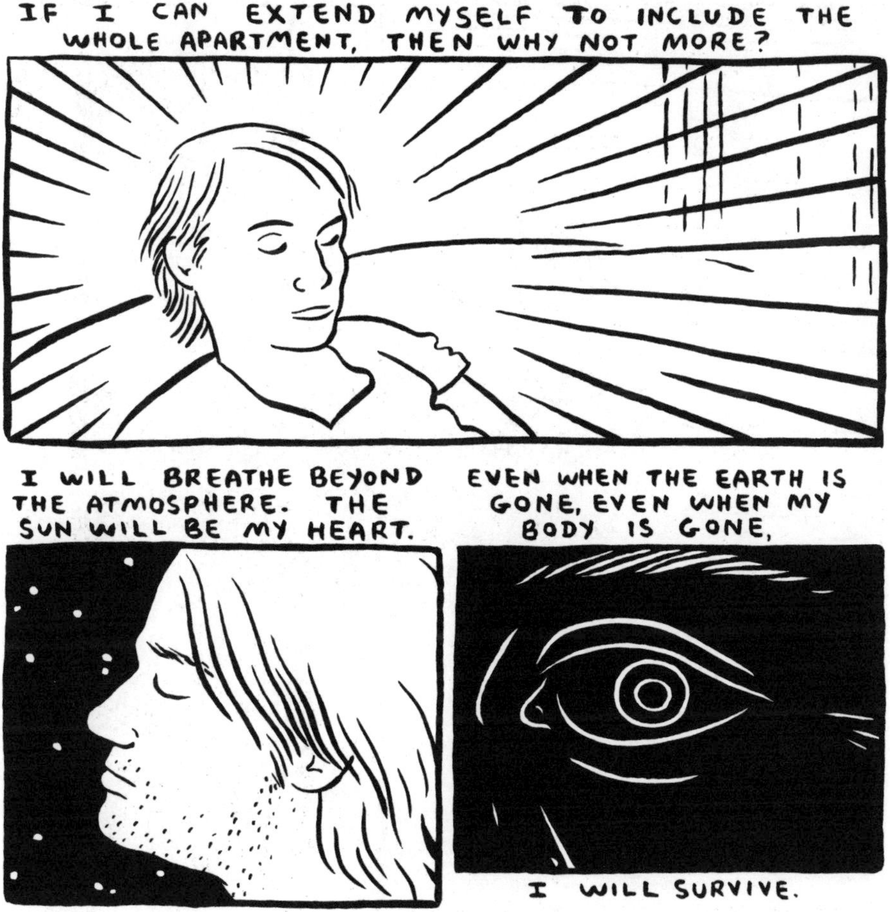
IF I CAN EXTEND MYSELF TO INCLUDE THE WHOLE APARTMENT, THEN WHY NOT MORE?
I WILL BREATHE BEYOND THE ATMOSPHERE. THE SUN WILL BE MY HEART.
EVEN WHEN THE EARTH IS GONE, EVEN WHEN MY BODY IS GONE,
I WILL SURVIVE.

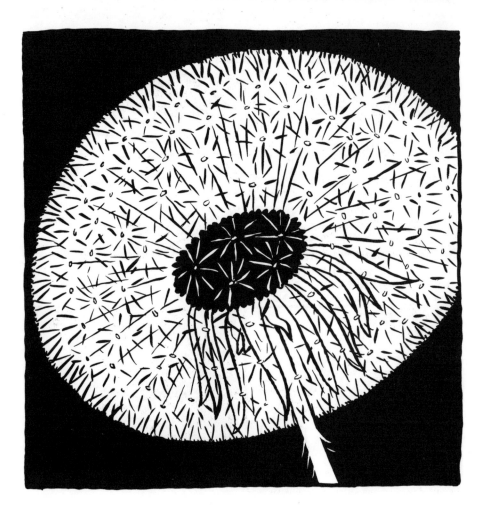

I WILL BE INFINITE, STRETCHING PAST PLUTO,
THROUGH THE COSMOS, TO NOTHING, AROUND & BACK AGAIN.

WILL I BE INFINITE?

I AM POWERLESS,

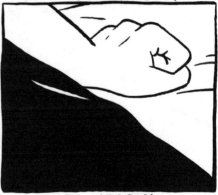

OR NEARLY.

I HAVE THE POWER TO GROW MY HAIR.
AND TO GROW MY FINGERNAILS
SLOWLY...
UNTIL THE SUN EXPLODES.

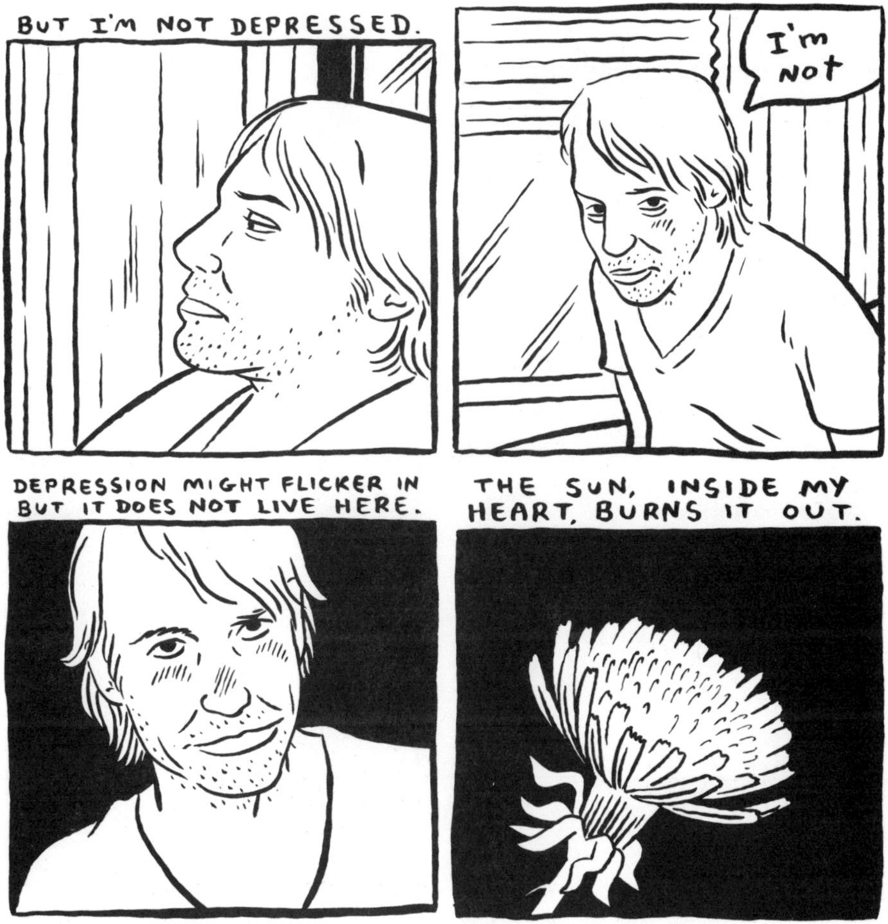
BUT I'M NOT DEPRESSED.
I'm not
DEPRESSION MIGHT FLICKER IN BUT IT DOES NOT LIVE HERE.
THE SUN, INSIDE MY HEART, BURNS IT OUT.

THE SUN THAT GREW
THE FLOWERS,

THAT GREW ME AND YOU,

WILL SWALLOW US ALL
ONE DAY...

ABSENTMINDEDLY.

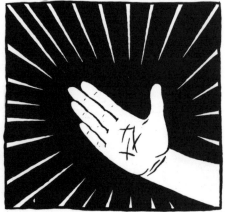

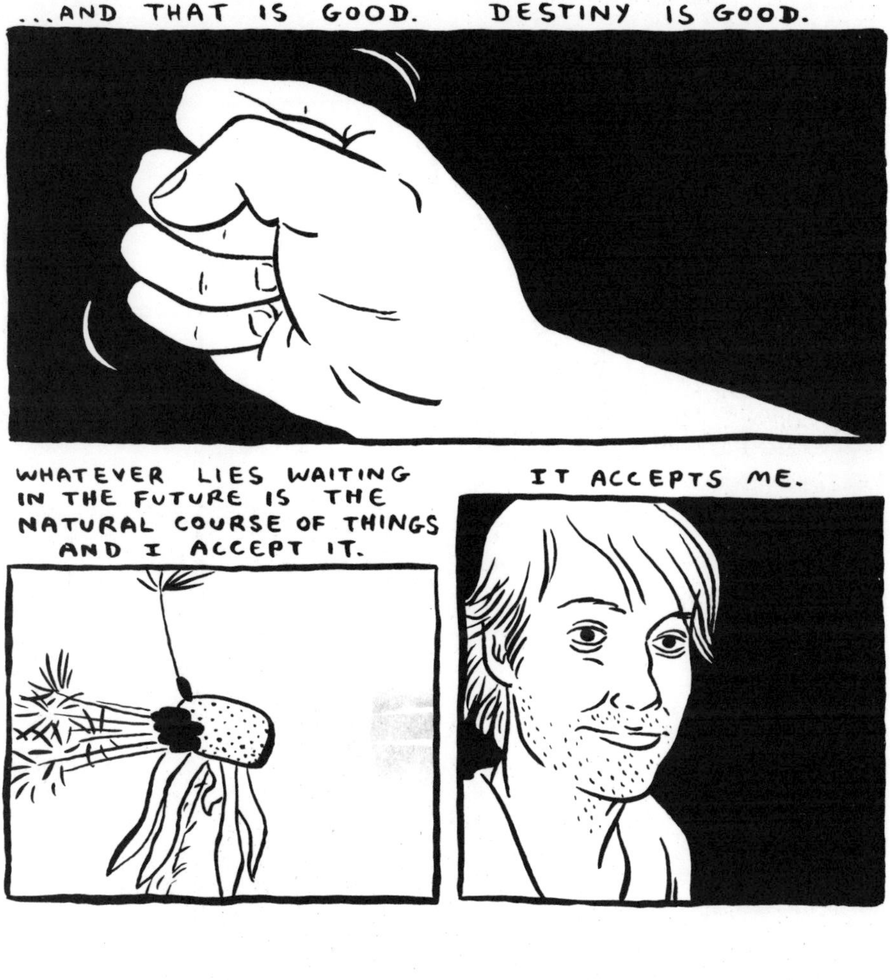
...AND THAT IS GOOD. DESTINY IS GOOD.
WHATEVER LIES WAITING IN THE FUTURE IS THE NATURAL COURSE OF THINGS AND I ACCEPT IT.
IT ACCEPTS ME.

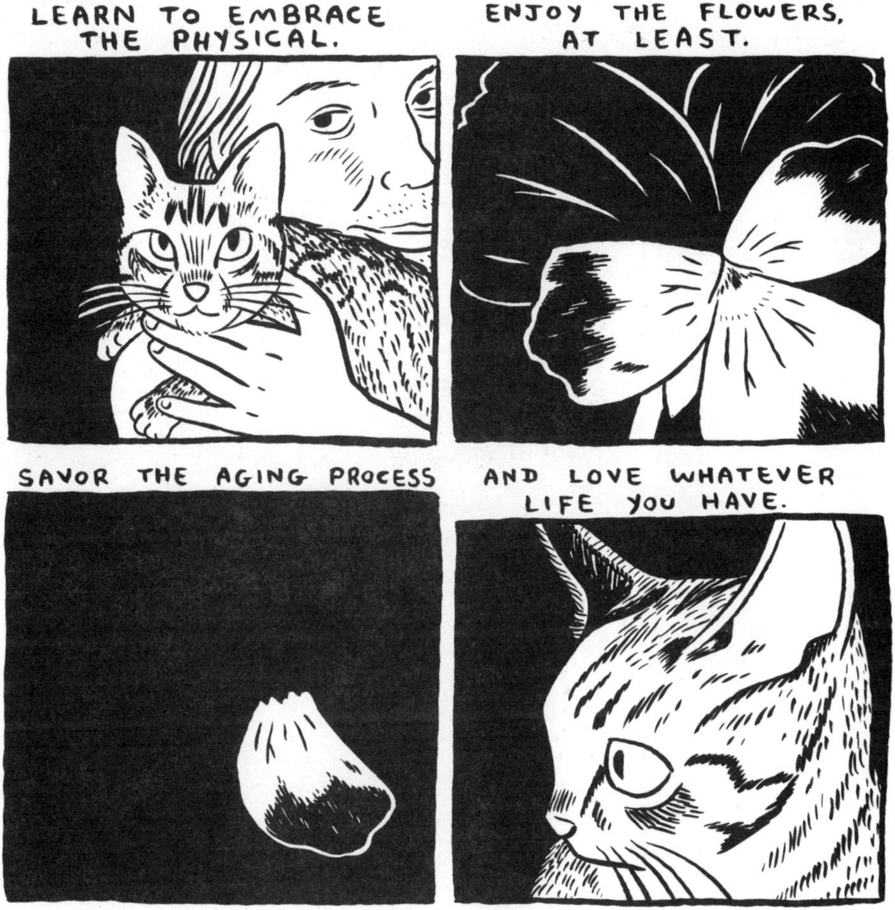
LEARN TO EMBRACE THE PHYSICAL.
ENJOY THE FLOWERS, AT LEAST.
SAVOR THE AGING PROCESS
AND LOVE WHATEVER LIFE YOU HAVE.

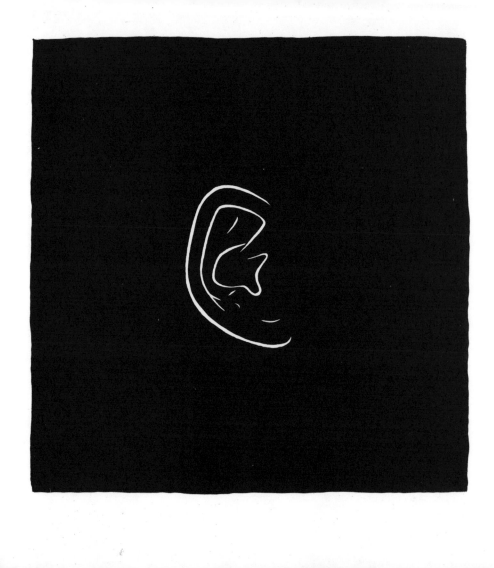

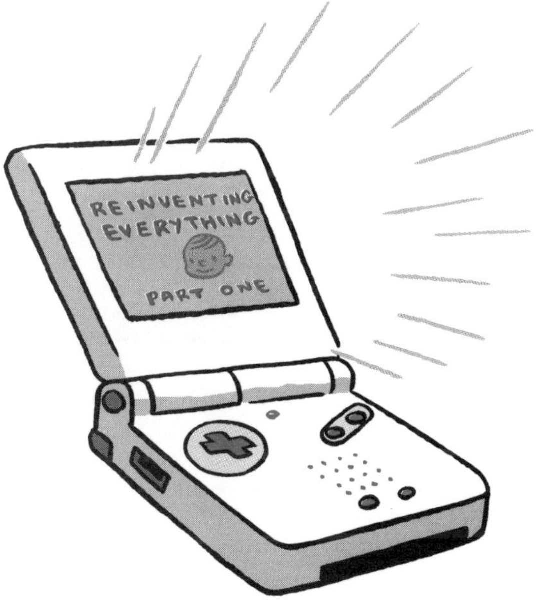
REINVENTING
EVERYTHING
PART ONE

PLAYING GAMEBOY IN A STATE PARK IN SOUTH CAROLINA

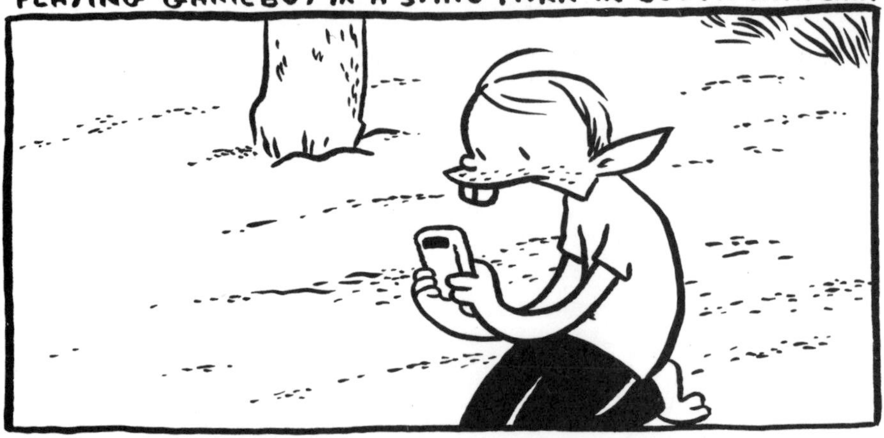

THE BEACH IS A GENTLE CURVE OF A SHAPE, LOW AND SERENE, AND FRINGED WITH PALM TREES

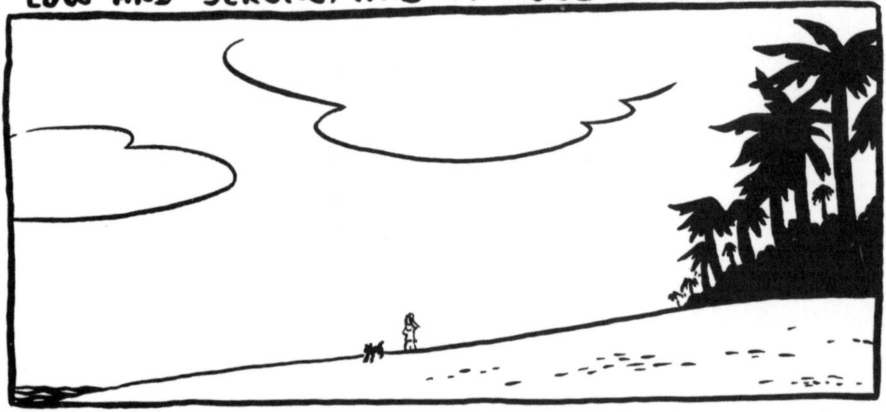

THIS GENTLE SHAPE, HOWEVER, IS MADE UP OF BILLIONS OF TINY BITS OF HARD SAND. A STRONG WIND PICKS UP THESE BITS AND WHIPS THEM ALONG THE SHORE. THEY STING MY SKIN AND I SQUEEZE MY EYES SHUT.

EVERYTHING IS MADE OUT OF TINY LITTLE BITS, I GUESS. MOLECULES, ATOMS, ELECTRONS, AND SMALLER AND SMALLER.

THE BEACH, THE TREES, EVEN THE CLOUDS IN THE SKY... EVERYTHING IS BUILT FROM LITTLE TINY PIECES OF STUFF.

JUST LIKE IN A GAMEBOY GAME... A NICE TIGHT LITTLE WORLD... AND ALL ITS INHABITANTS... MADE OUT OF LITTLE BUILDING BLOCKS.

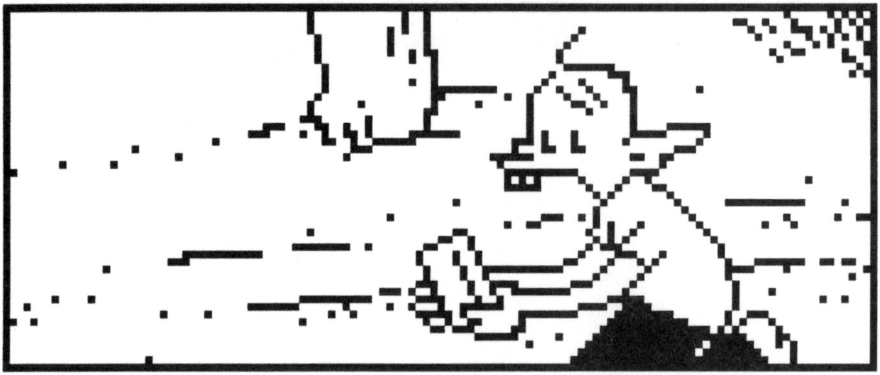

ART SIMPLIFIES AND FOCUSES THE WORLD AROUND US, CONDENSING EXPERIENCE INTO MORE EASILY DEFINABLE SHAPES. EVEN THE MOST COMPLICATED WORK OF ART IS A VAST SIMPLIFICATION OF THE ACTUAL WORLD IN WHICH WE LIVE.

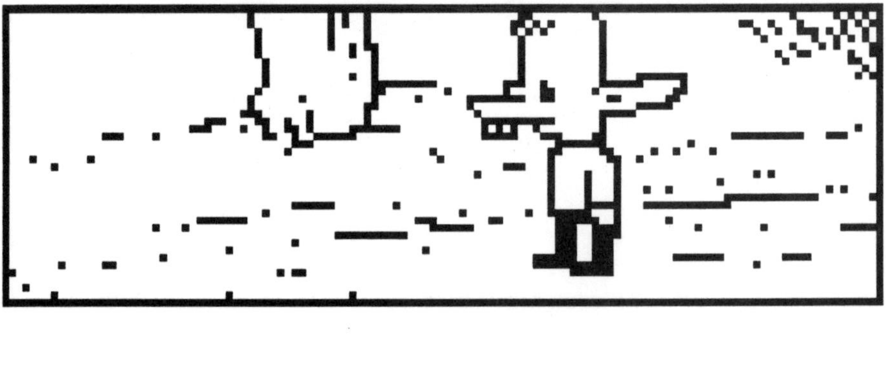

HOWEVER... THIS SIMPLIFICATION UNFOLDS IN OUR MINDS AS A GREAT EXPANSION.

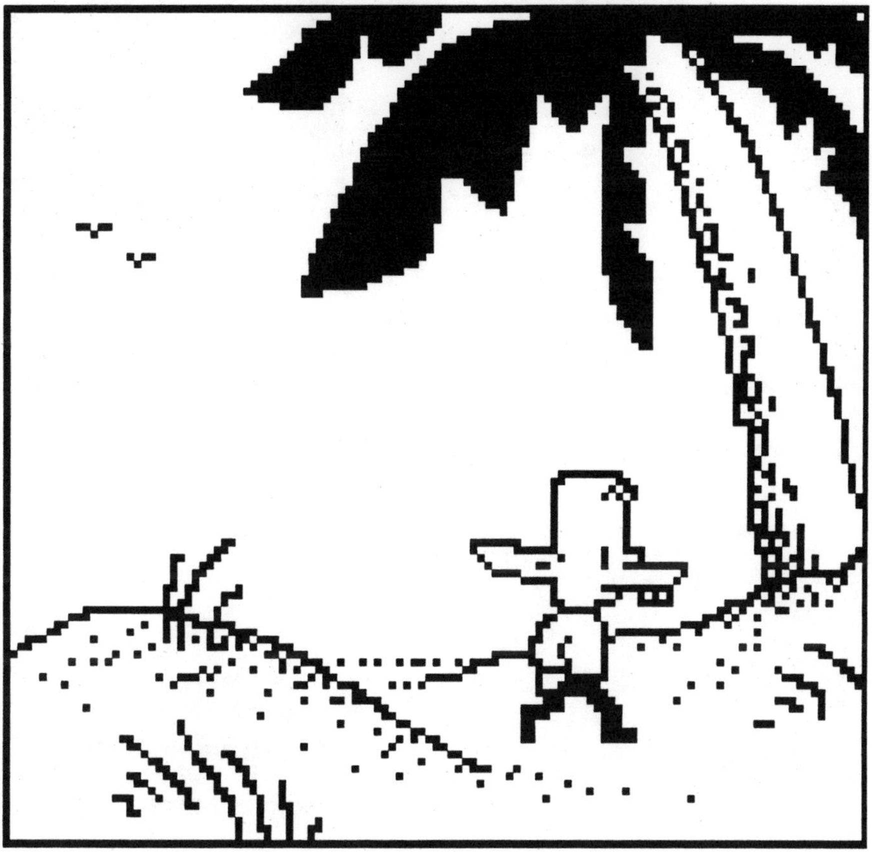

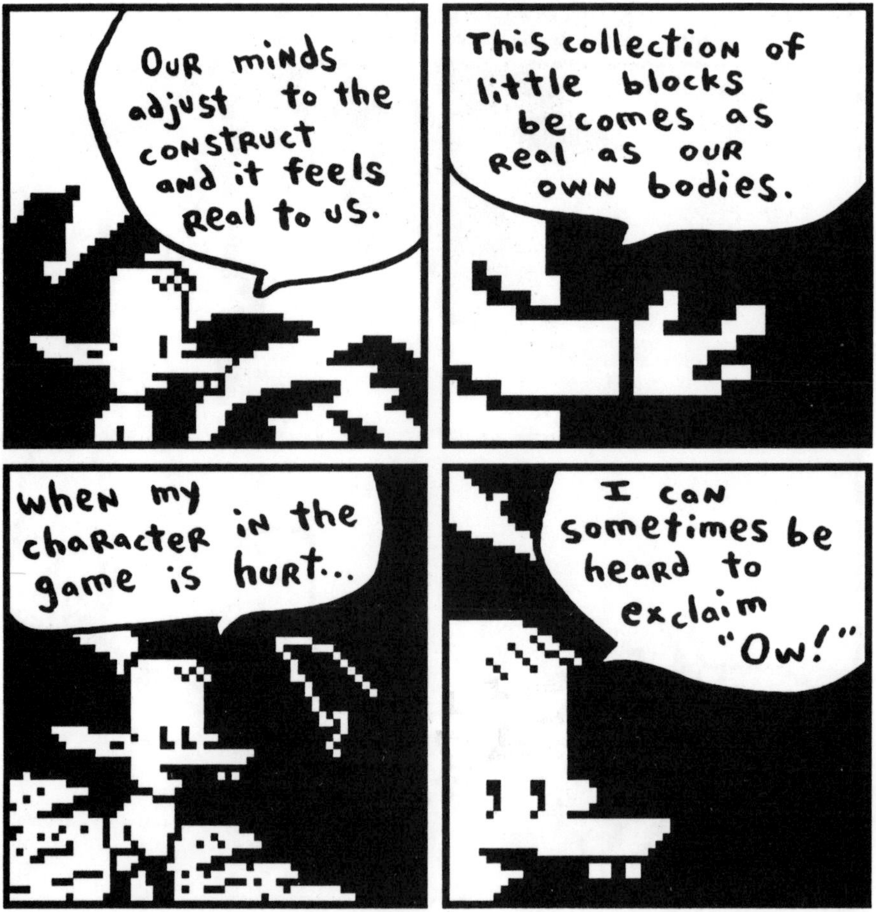
Our minds adjust to the construct and it feels real to us.
This collection of little blocks becomes as real as our own bodies.
When my character in the game is hurt...
I can sometimes be heard to exclaim "Ow!"

trip
Ow!
bloop
There's an incredibly strong connection between the "player" and the "game"
This is the kind of visceral impact that painters can only dream of eliciting with their work.

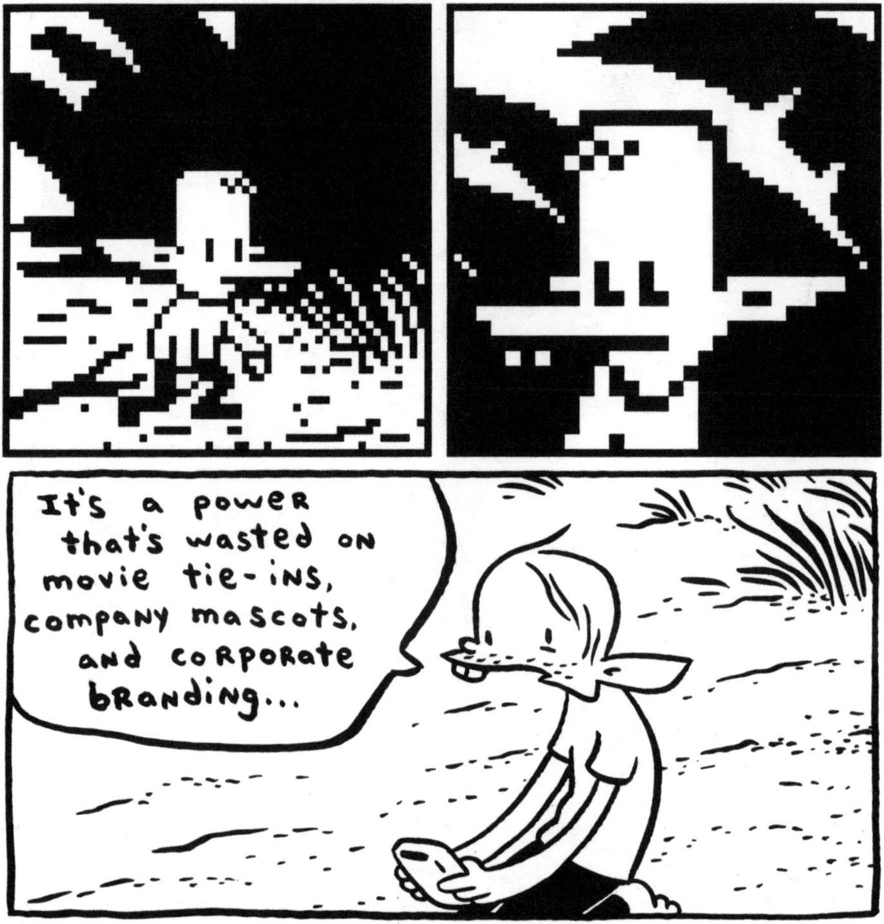
It's a power that's wasted on movie tie-ins, company mascots, and corporate branding...

why can't these little pixels be the building blocks for love..?
for loss
for understanding?

WE'RE CONSTANTLY BOMBARDED WITH MEANINGLESS BITS OF INFORMATION AND EMPTY PIXELS, EMAILS WITH HALF-WRITTEN SENTENCES, STUPID OLD POP SONGS BROKEN INTO "SAMPLES" AND PIECED TOGETHER INTO EVEN STUPIDER NEW POP SONGS, INSTANT MESSENGER, CELL PHONES, WALKMANS, LAPTOPS, AND WHATEVER NEW IS ON THE HORIZON. WE'RE ALWAYS PLUGGED IN TO SOMETHING.

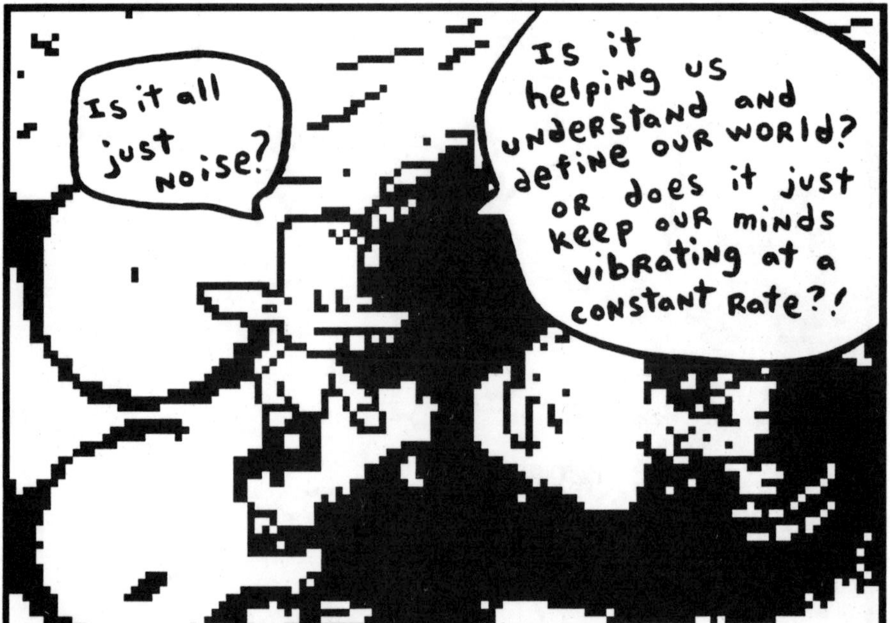

Is it all just noise?
Is it helping us understand and define our world? or does it just keep our minds vibrating at a constant Rate?!

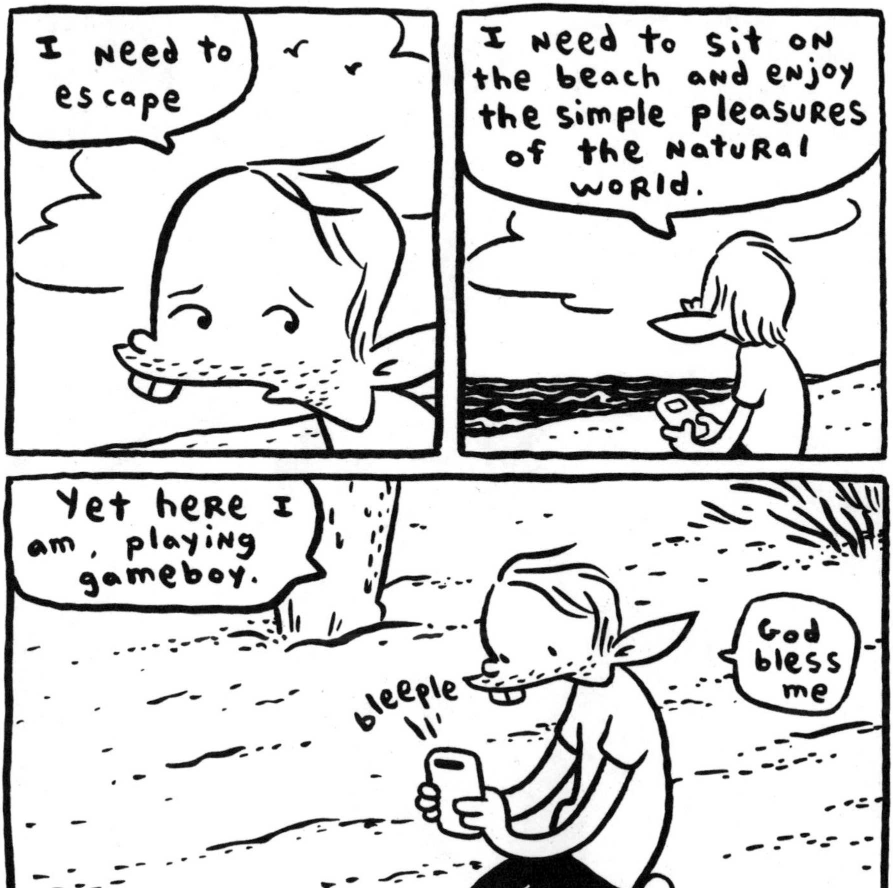
I need to escape
I need to sit on the beach and enjoy the simple pleasures of the natural world.
Yet here I am, playing gameboy.
bleeple
God bless me

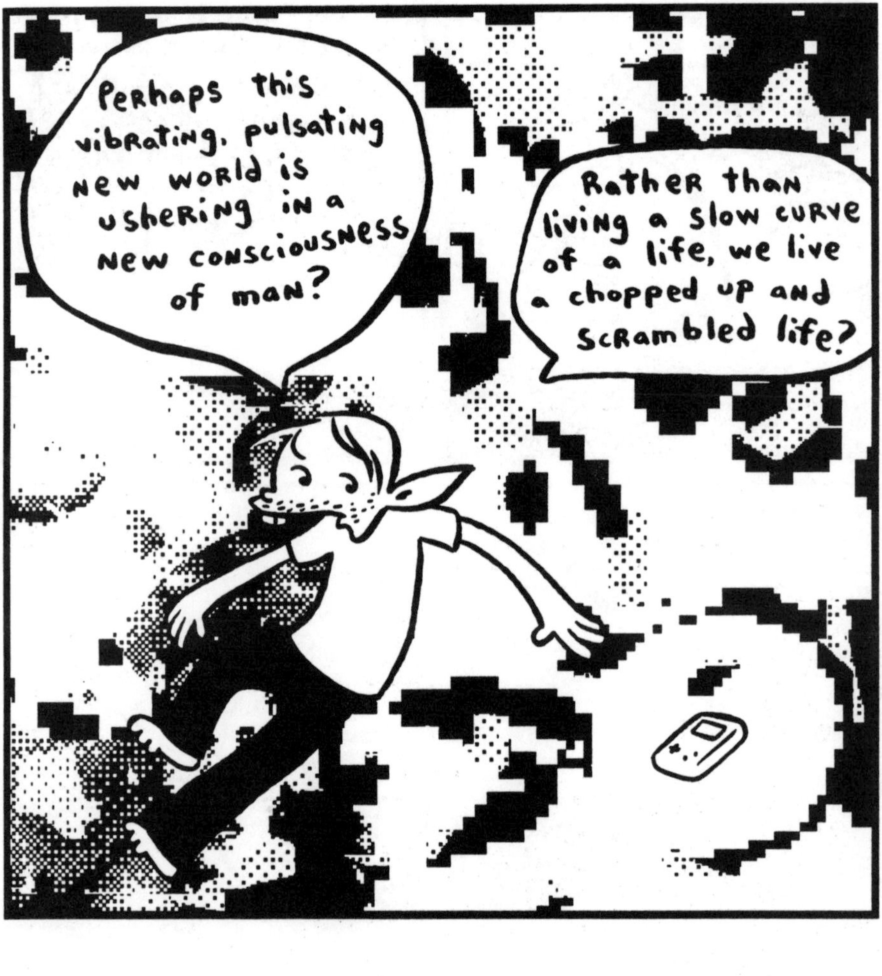
Perhaps this vibrating, pulsating new world is ushering in a new consciousness of man?
Rather than living a slow curve of a life, we live a chopped up and scrambled life?

ACTUALLY, EVEN THE SLOWEST, CALMEST DAYS HAVE ALWAYS TEEMED WITH ACTIVITY. MICRORGANISMS SECRETLY SQUIRMING.

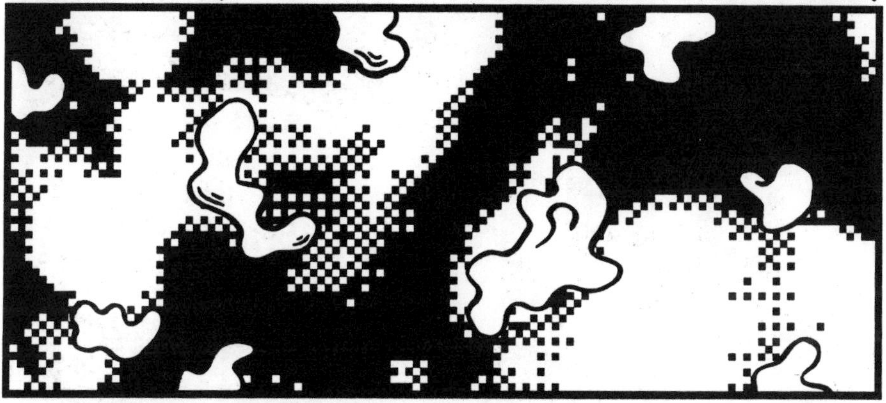

COUNTLESS UNKNOWN HUMAN BIRTHS & DEATHS OCCUR AROUND THE GLOBE IN THE BLINK OF AN EYE.

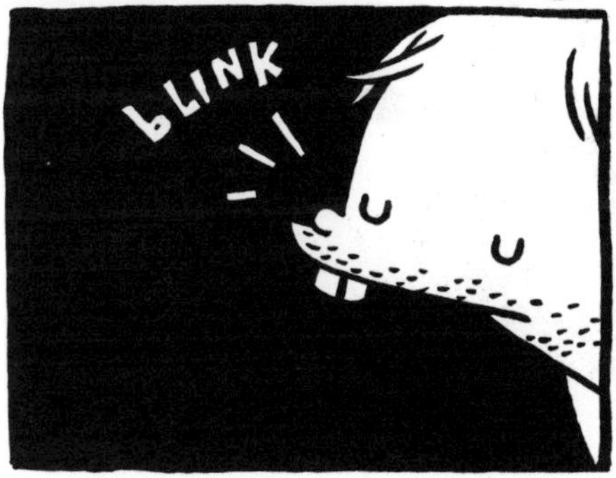
BLINK

WHAT'S MORE, WE'RE ACTUALLY AWARE OF ALL THIS FRENZIED ACTIVITY, AND WE TRY TO CRAM THIS INFINITY OF EXPERIENCE INTO OUR DAILY LIVES.

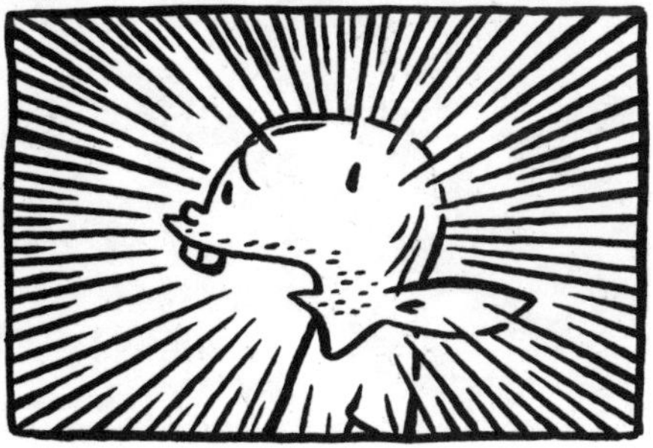

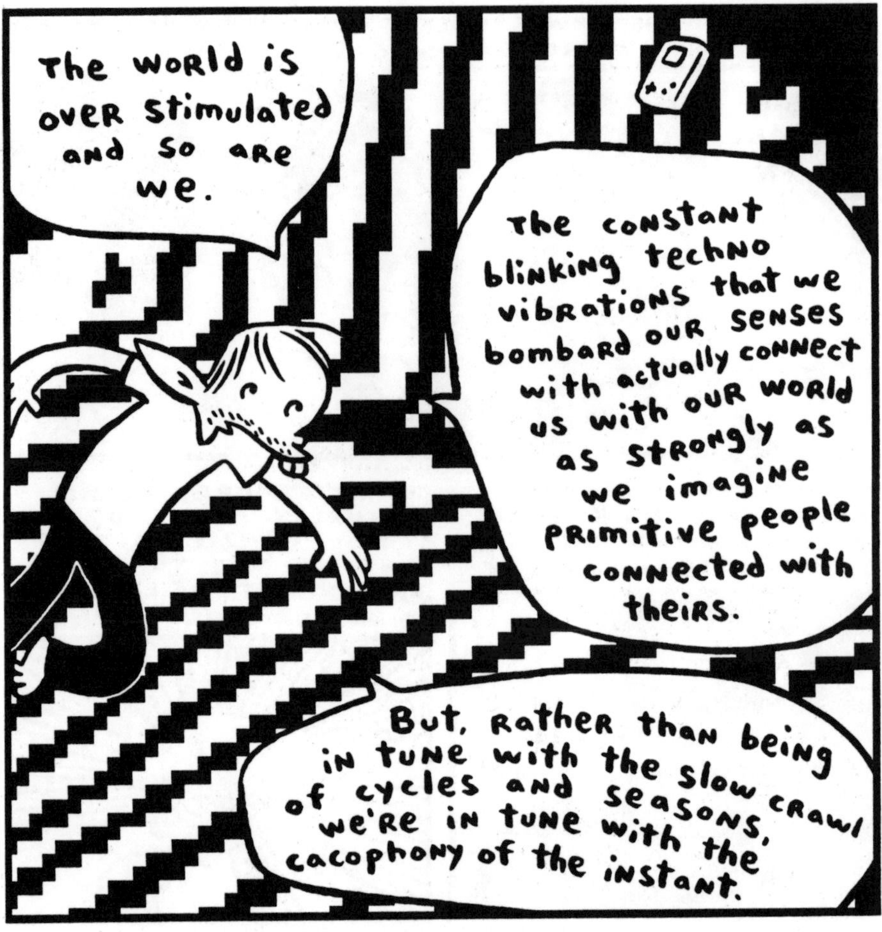
The world is over stimulated and so are we.
The constant blinking techno vibrations that we bombard our senses with actually connect us with our world as strongly as we imagine primitive people connected with theirs.
But, rather than being in tune with the slow crawl of cycles and seasons, we're in tune with the cacophony of the instant.

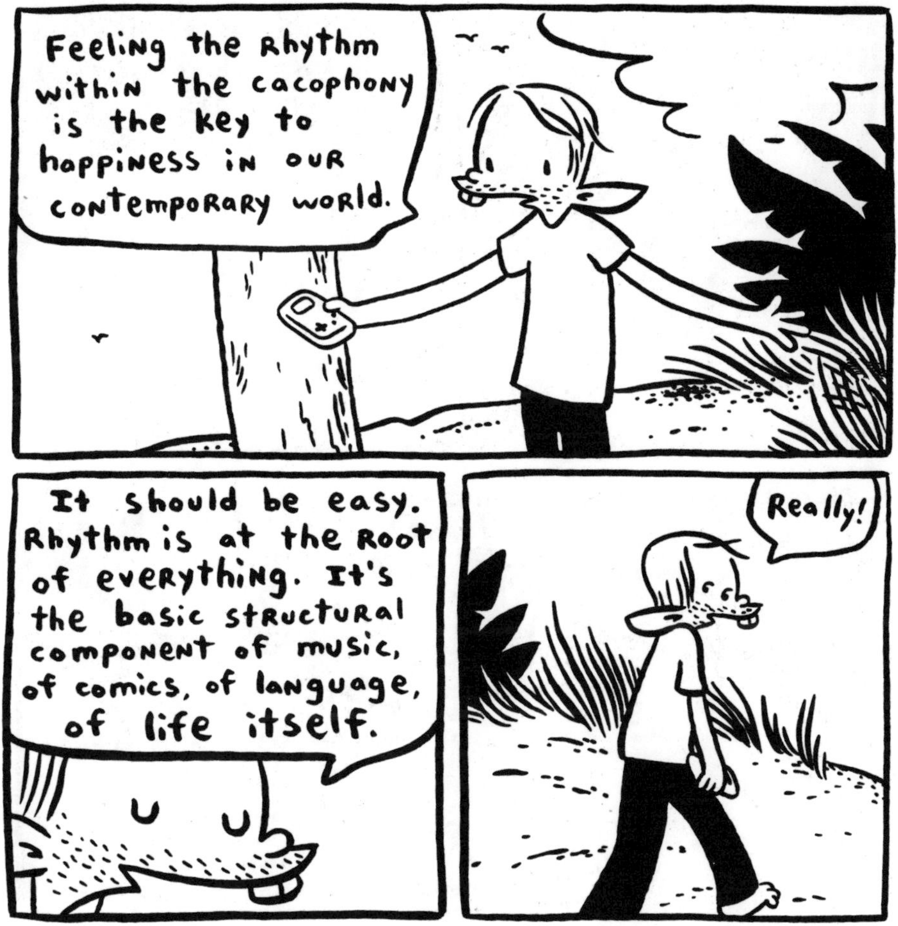
Feeling the rhythm within the cacophony is the key to happiness in our contemporary world.
It should be easy. Rhythm is at the root of everything. It's the basic structural component of music, of comics, of language, of life itself.
Really!

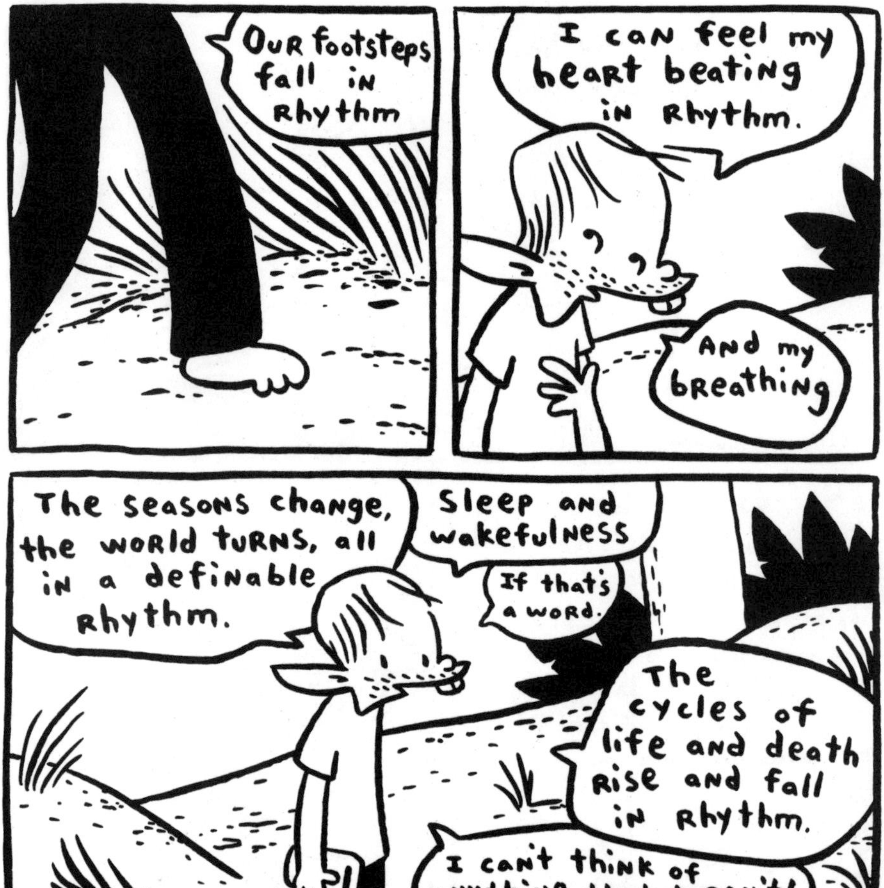
Our footsteps fall in rhythm
I can feel my heart beating in rhythm.
And my breathing
The seasons change, the world turns, all in a definable rhythm.
Sleep and wakefulness
If that's a word.
The cycles of life and death rise and fall in rhythm.
I can't think of anything that doesn't!

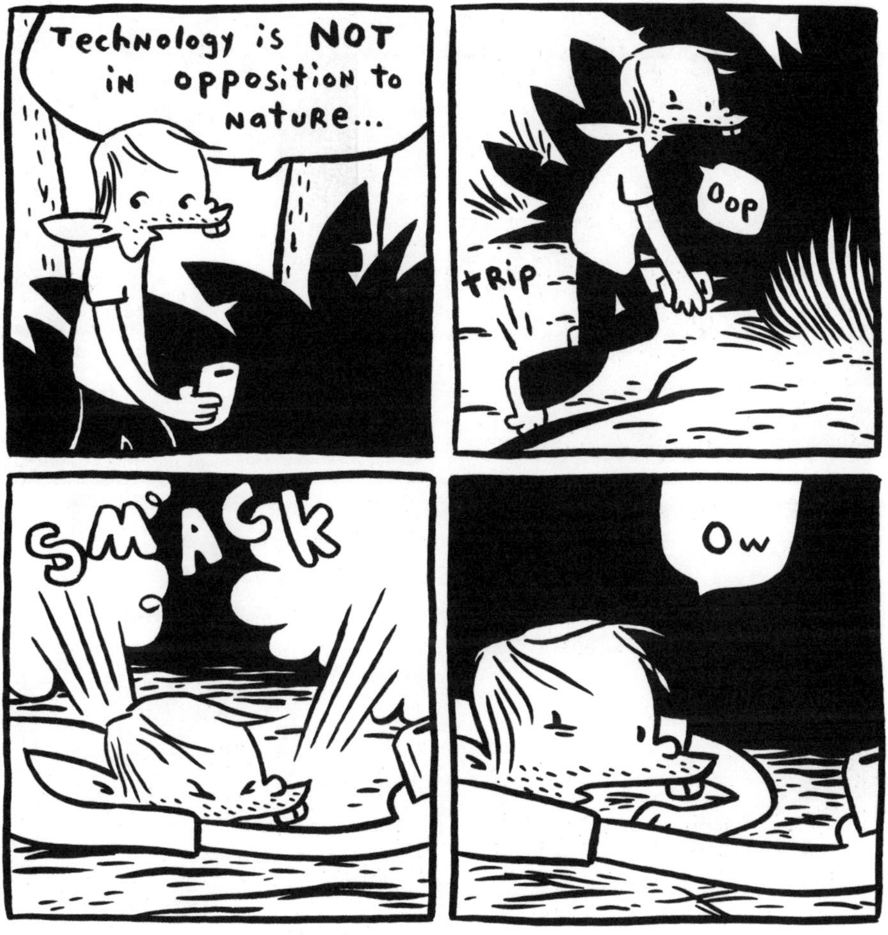
Technology is NOT in opposition to nature...
OOP
TRIP
SMACK
Ow

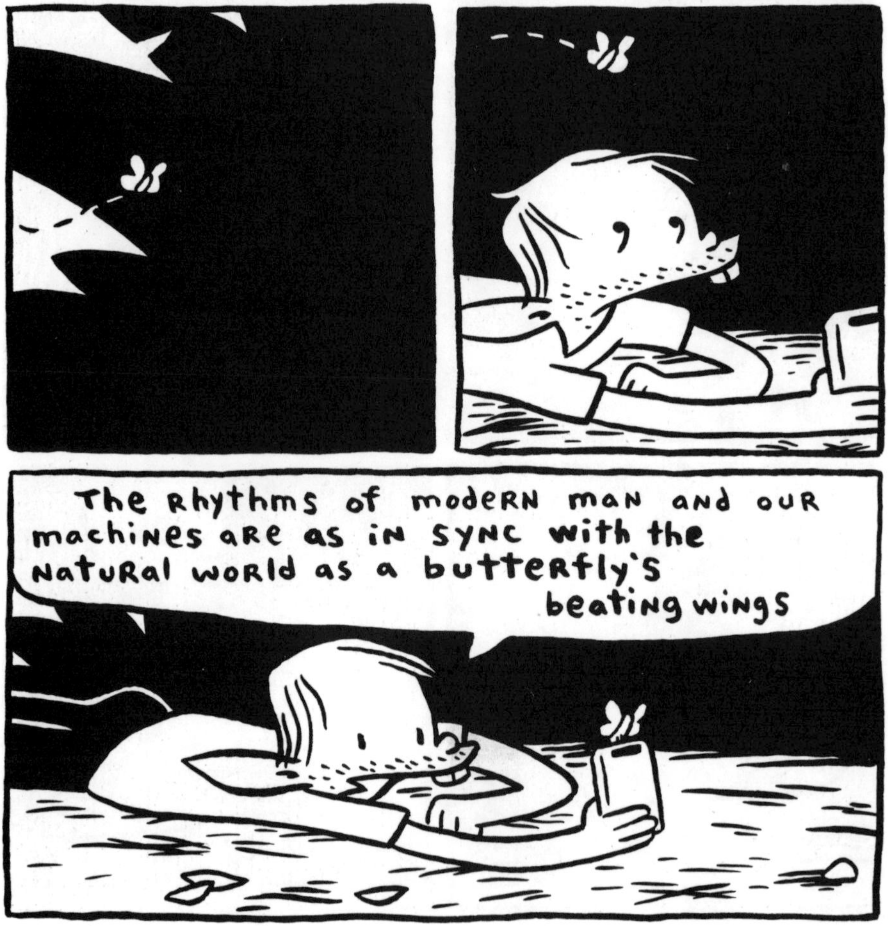
The rhythms of modern man and our machines are as in sync with the natural world as a butterfly's beating wings

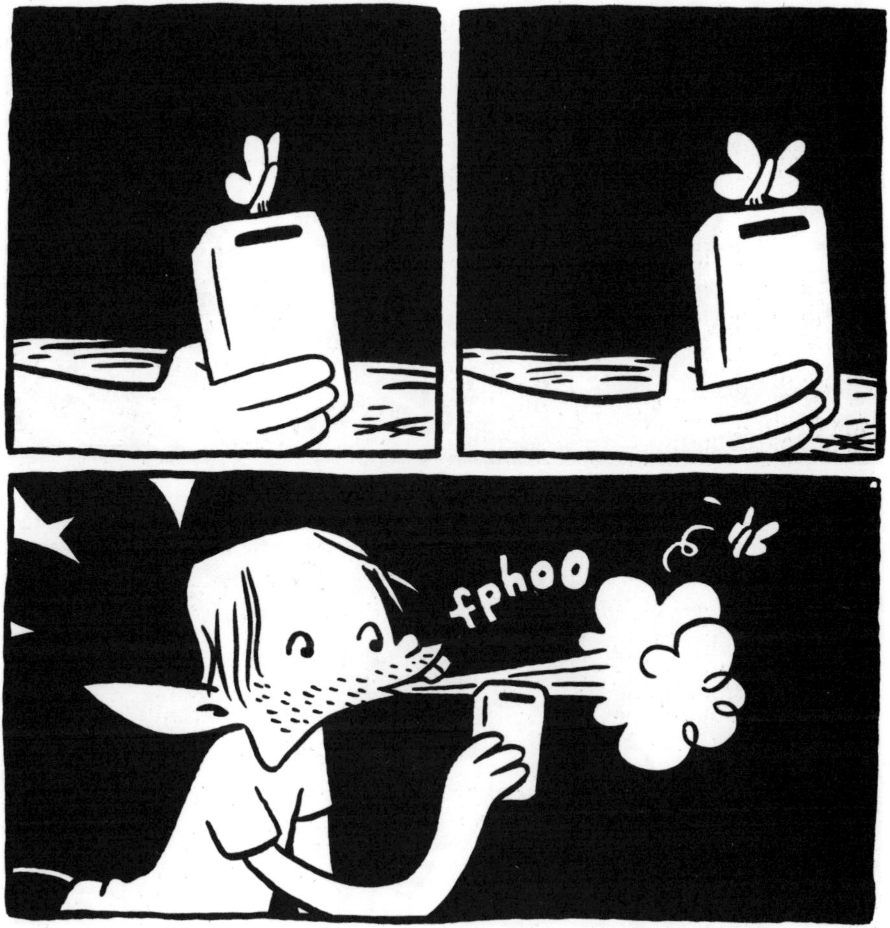
fphoo

ACCEPT THE BEAUTY IN EVERYTHING.

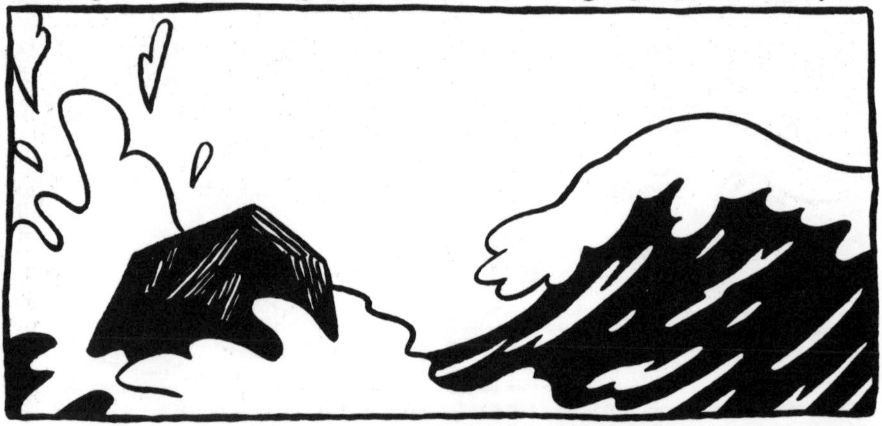

WAVES CRASHING AGAINST THE SHORE
OR SMOKESTACKS BELCHING SOUR CLOUDS.

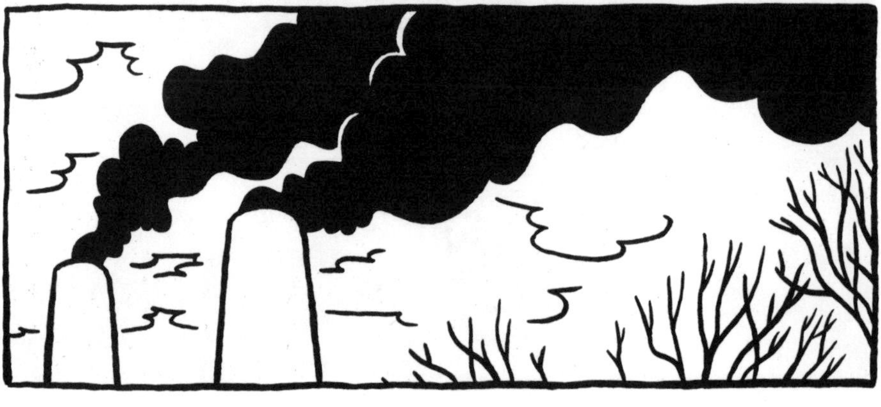

STUMBLING BABY KITTENS OR EXPLODING BUILDINGS.

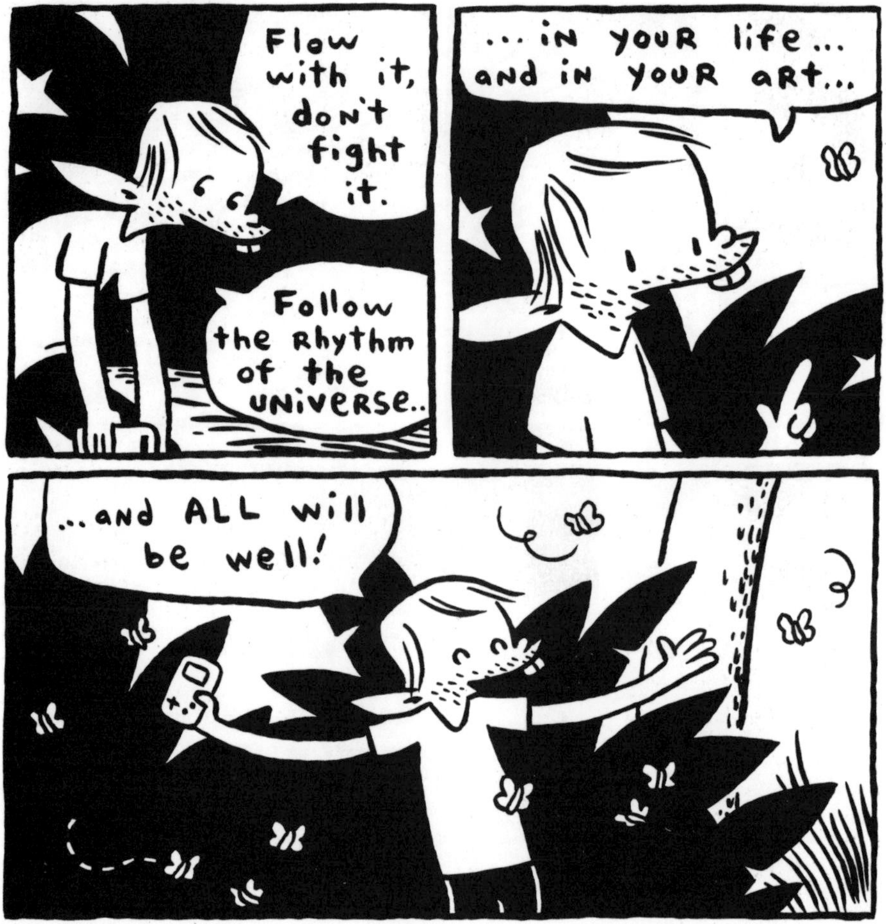
Flow with it, don't fight it.
Follow the Rhythm of the universe..
...in your life... and in your art...
...and ALL will be well!

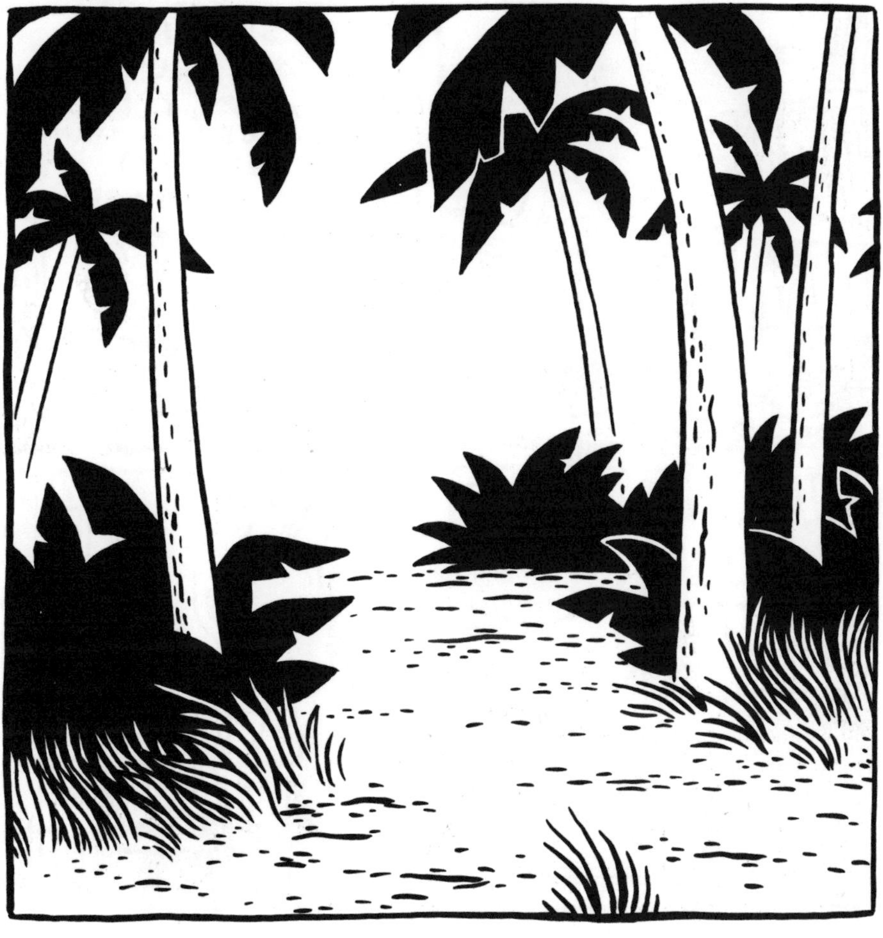

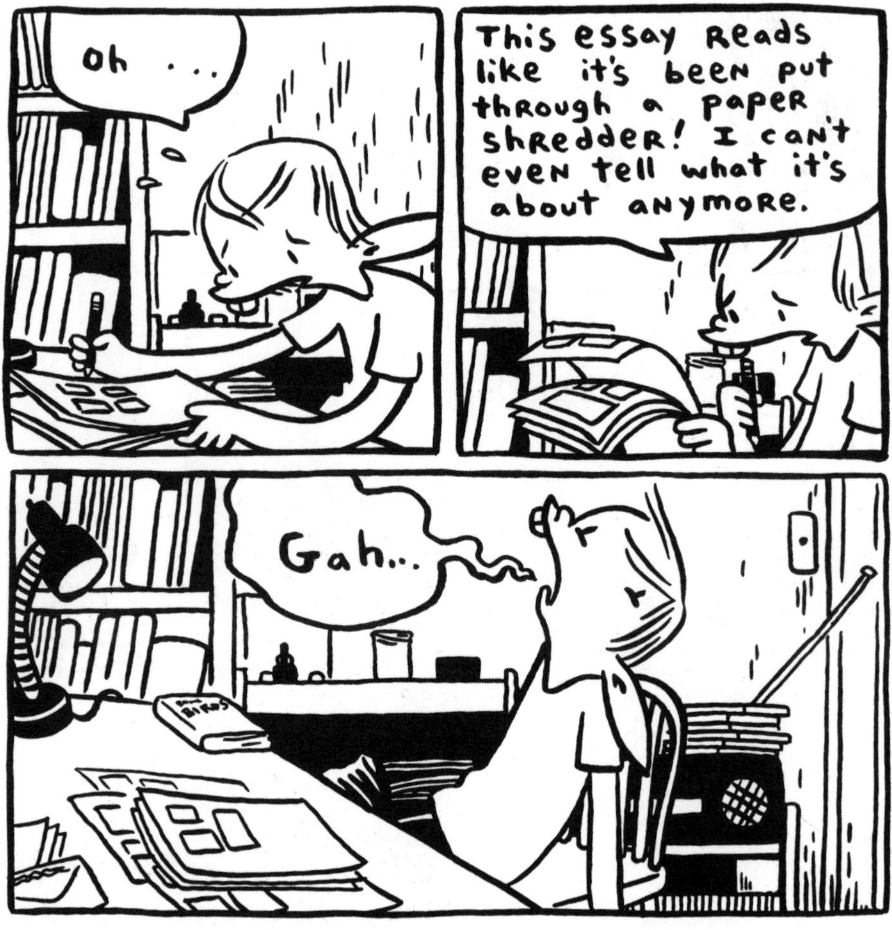
Oh ...
This essay reads like it's been put through a paper shredder! I can't even tell what it's about anymore.
Gah...

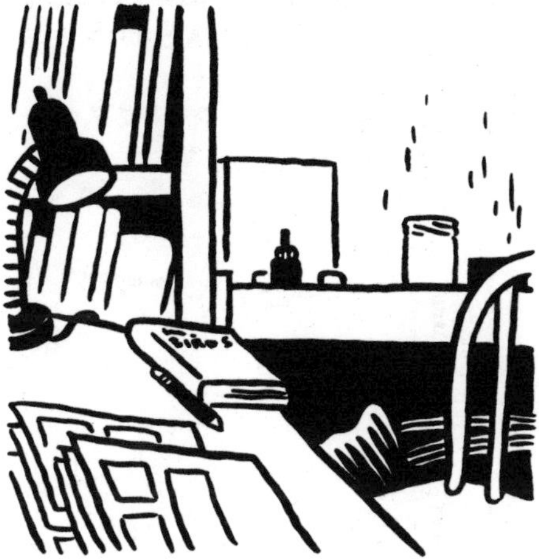
BIRDS

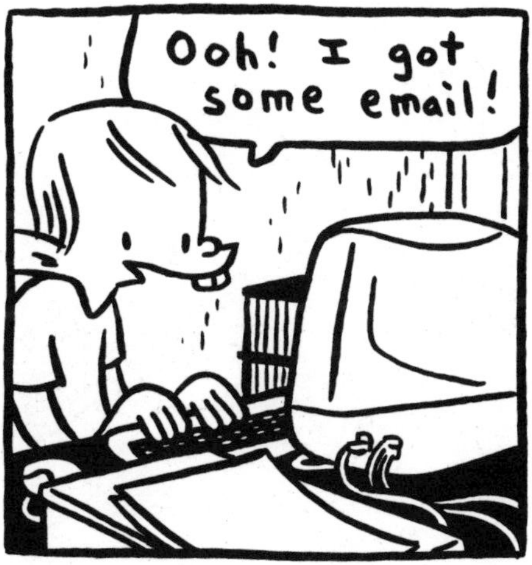
Ooh! I got some email!

# REINVENTING EVERYTHING

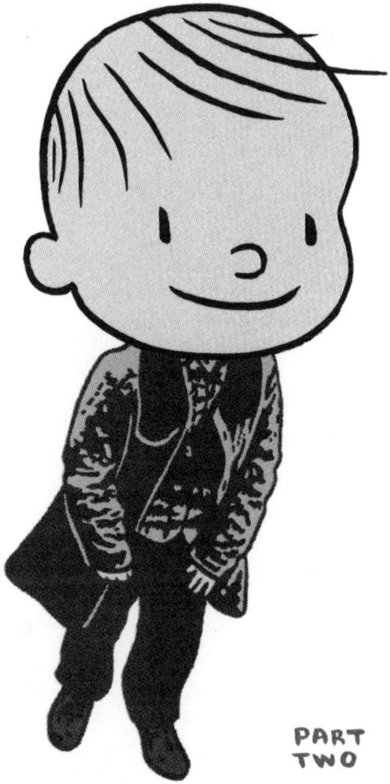

PART TWO

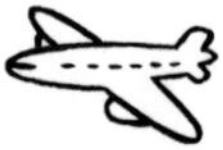

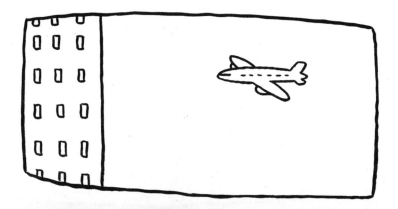

REINVENTING
EVERYTHING

TWO PLANES KNOCKED DOWN TWO TOWERS. IT WAS A MASSIVE BLOW. THE SHOCK BLEW STRAIGHT THROUGH US.

IT WAS DIFFICULT TO COMPREHEND WHAT HAD HAPPENED.

A BIT OF MY "SOUL" HAD BEEN BLASTED OUT AND NOW THERE WAS A TINY EMPTY PLACE INSIDE ME.

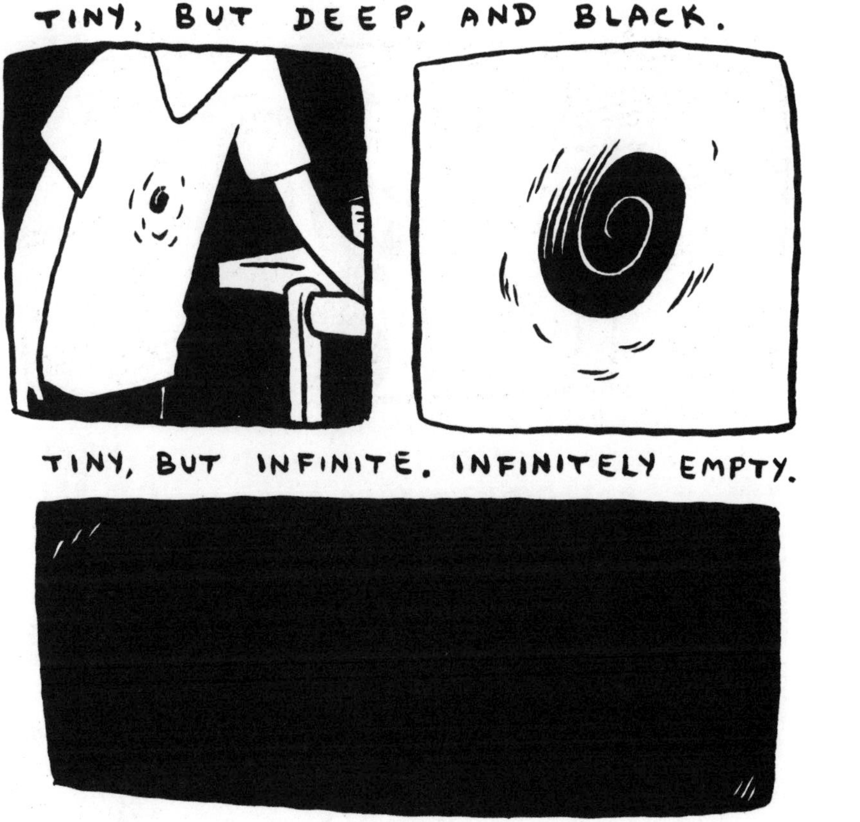
TINY, BUT DEEP, AND BLACK.
TINY, BUT INFINITE. INFINITELY EMPTY.

HOWEVER, AFTER A PERIOD OF NOTHING, SOMETHING HAPPENED IN THE VOID. A TINY IDEA TOOK FORM OF ITS OWN VOLITION.

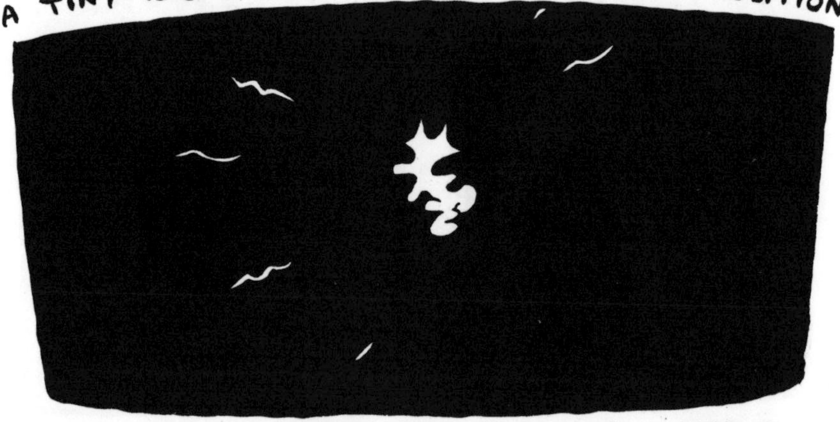

AN IDEA THAT I COULDN'T SHAKE, THAT FOLLOWED ME EVERY DAY, ALL DAY LONG, FOR OVER A YEAR...

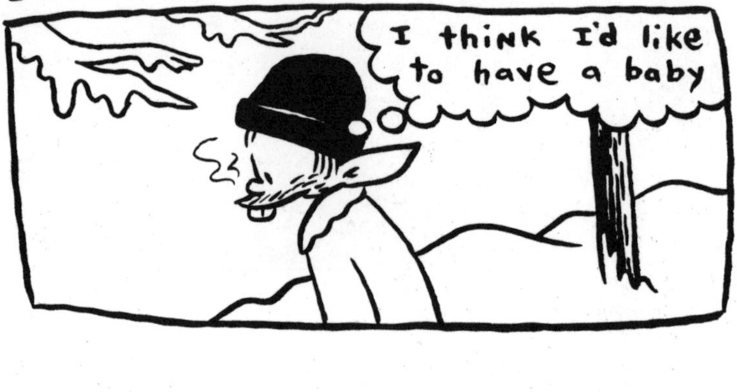
I think I'd like to have a baby

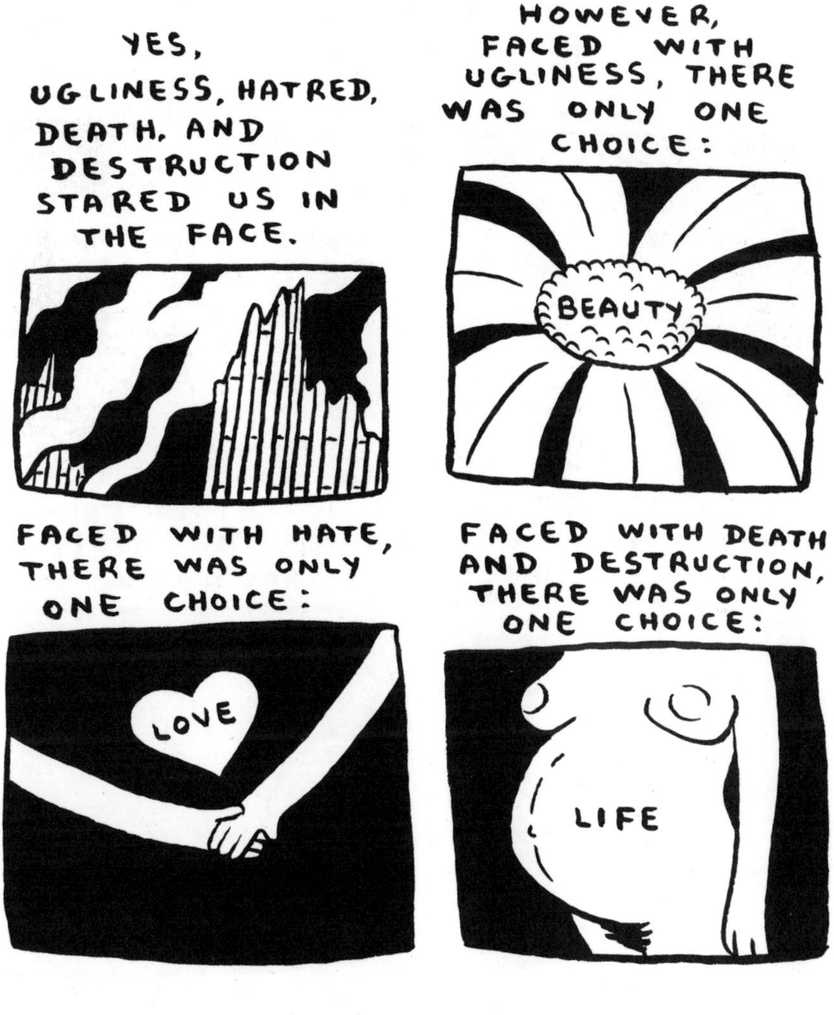
YES,
UGLINESS, HATRED, DEATH, AND DESTRUCTION STARED US IN THE FACE.
HOWEVER, FACED WITH UGLINESS, THERE WAS ONLY ONE CHOICE:
BEAUTY
FACED WITH HATE, THERE WAS ONLY ONE CHOICE:
LOVE
FACED WITH DEATH AND DESTRUCTION, THERE WAS ONLY ONE CHOICE:
LIFE

WE DECIDED TO HAVE A BABY...

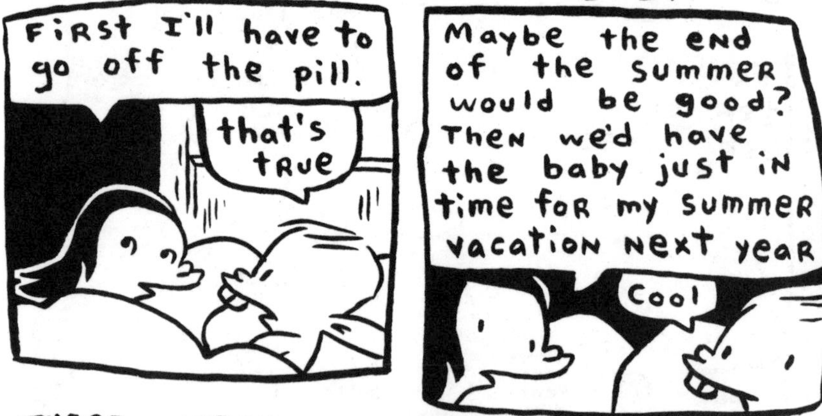
First I'll have to go off the pill.
that's true
Maybe the end of the summer would be good? Then we'd have the baby just in time for my summer vacation next year
Cool

THERE WERE REASONS NOT TO.
WE'D BE GIVING UP A LOT OF FREEDOM THAT WE'D ENJOYED AS A COUPLE.
WE'D BEEN SWEETHEARTS FOR A LONG TIME.*

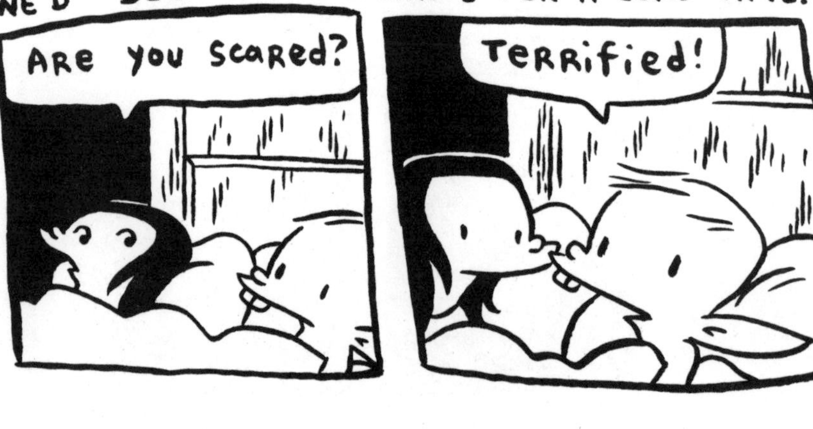
Are you scared?
Terrified!

* SEVENTEEN YEARS

OUR LIVES WOULD CHANGE FOREVER, BUT THAT'S BETTER THAN STAGNATION.

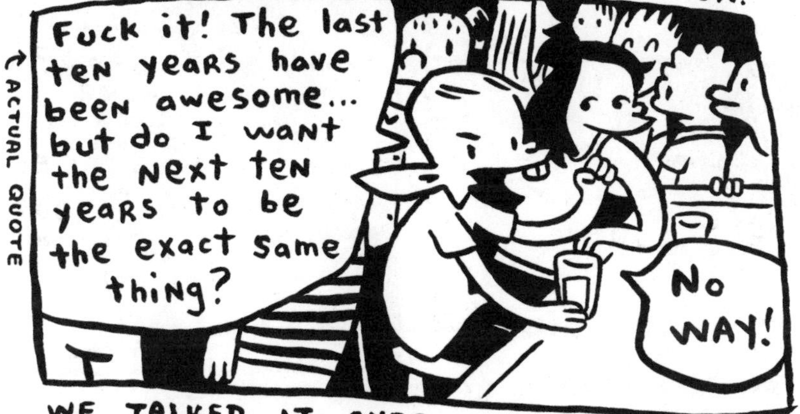
Fuck it! The last ten years have been awesome... but do I want the next ten years to be the exact same thing?
No WAY!
ACTUAL QUOTE

WE TALKED IT OVER A LOT, WEIGHED THE PROS AND CONS, BUT IT WAS REALLY BEYOND OUR CHOOSING. HE BEGAN AS A SPARK OF AN IDEA, AND THEN THE SPARK CAUGHT OUR THOUGHTS ON FIRE. IT'S LIKE HE WAS WILLING HIMSELF INTO EXISTENCE.

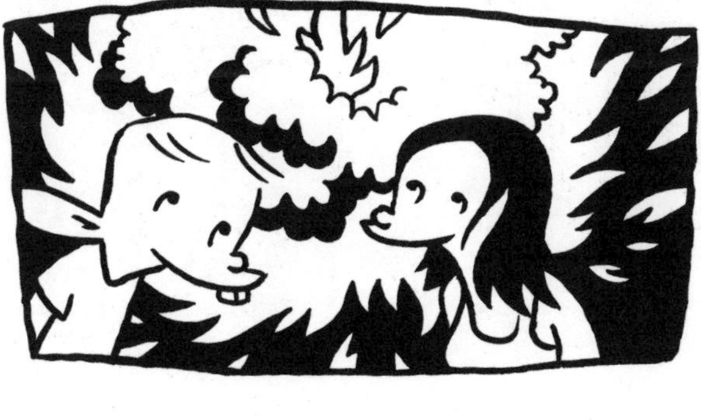

I KNEW THAT AS HIS FIRE WOULD RAGE, SO WOULD OUR OLD LIVES BE BURNED AWAY.

SO WHY NOT GO OUT IN A BLAZE OF GLORY? WE PARTIED HARD THAT SUMMER, AS IF WE WERE SAYING GOODBYE TO OURSELVES. RIDING BIKES DRUNK AT 4:00 AM WITH MY EYES CLOSED FELT LIKE THE ULTIMATE FREEDOM.

THEN WE MADE THAT BABY REAL. SOMETHING YOU MUST KNOW: THE TRANSFORMATION FROM IDEA TO PHYSICAL PRESENCE IS A WRENCHING ONE.

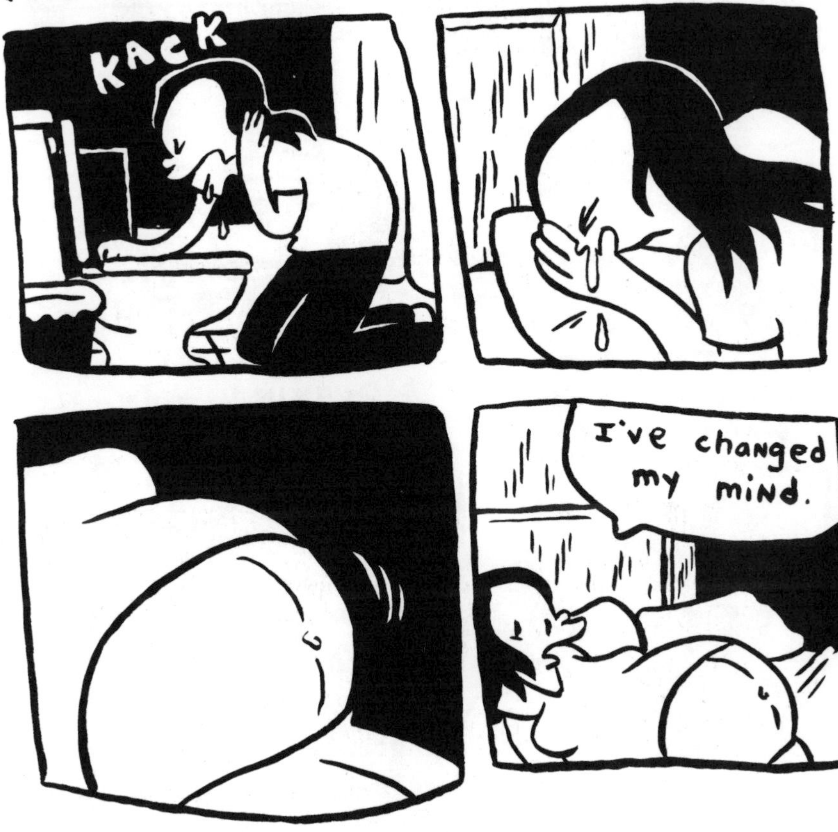
KACK
I've changed my mind.

THERE'S A LOT OF JOY IN THE EXPERIENCE, TOO.

CHOOSING NAMES:

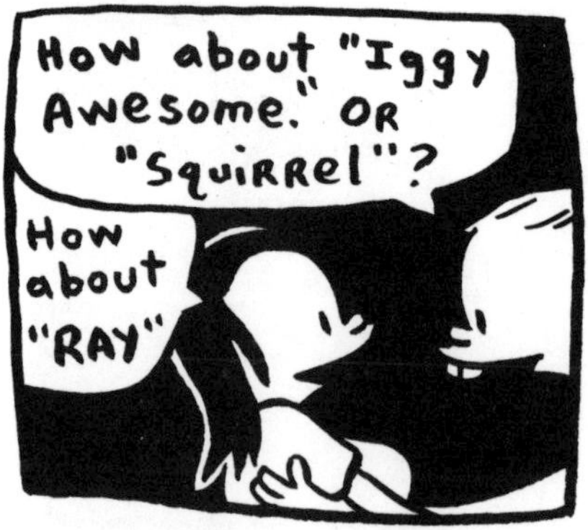
How about "Iggy Awesome." OR "Squirrel"?
How about "RAY"

SWIMMING:

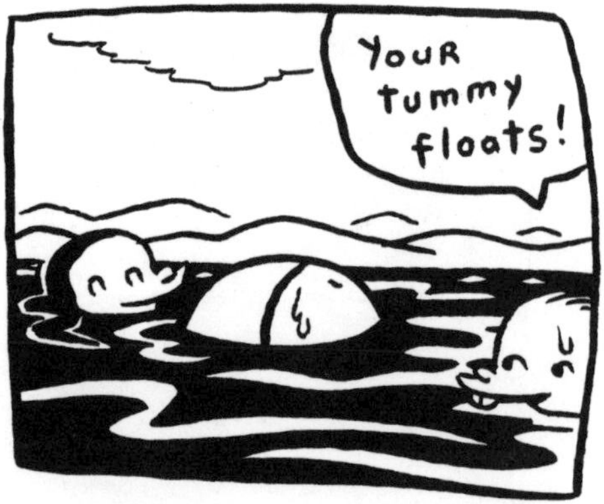
Your tummy floats!

WATCHING THE BABY KICK:

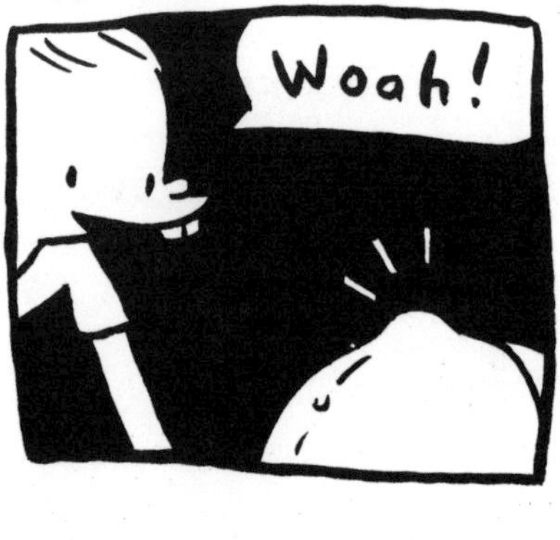
Woah!

TRYING OUT NEW SEXUAL POSITIONS

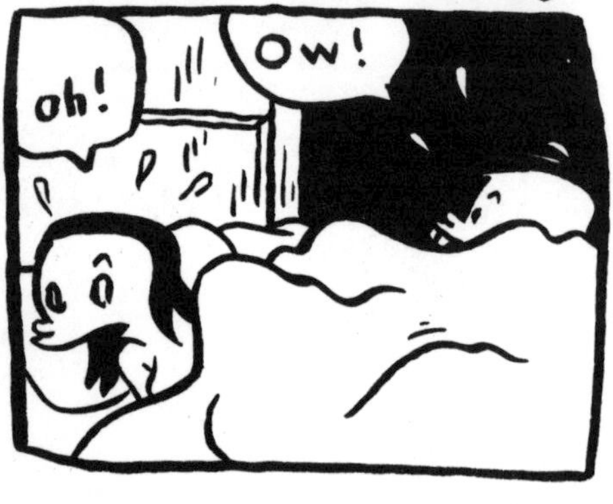
oh!
Ow!

WE HAD SO MUCH JUNK, SO MANY BOXES OF BOOKS, HOW COULD WE MAKE ROOM FOR A BABY IN THIS LITTLE APARTMENT?

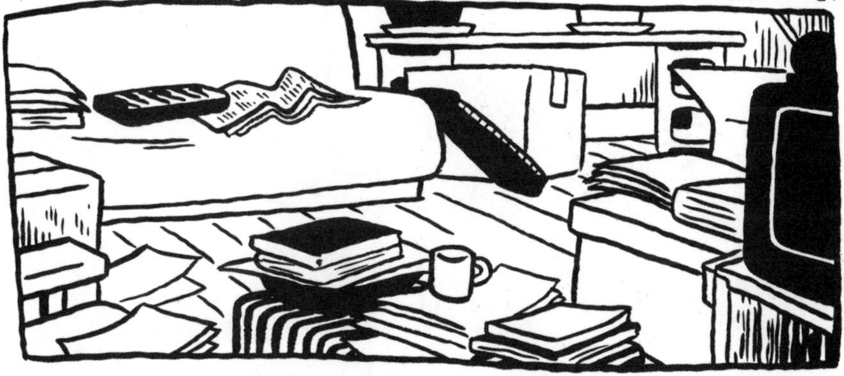

SO WE DECIDED TO BUY A HOUSE.

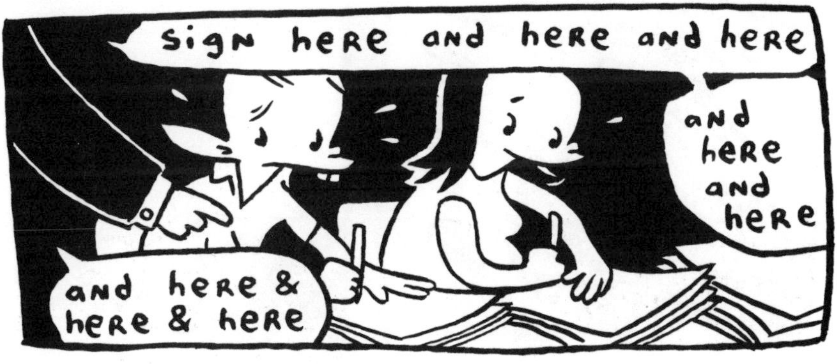
sign here and here and here
and here and here
and here & here & here

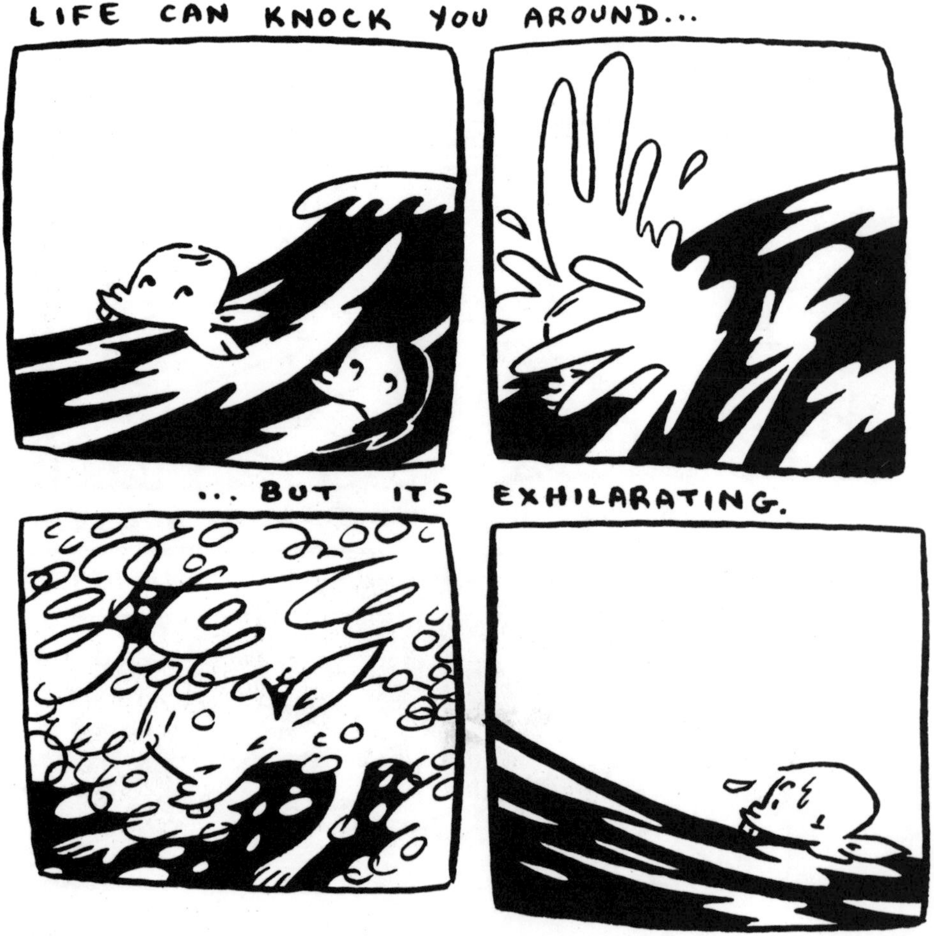
LIFE CAN KNOCK YOU AROUND...
... BUT ITS EXHILARATING.

DON'T FIGHT LIFE!

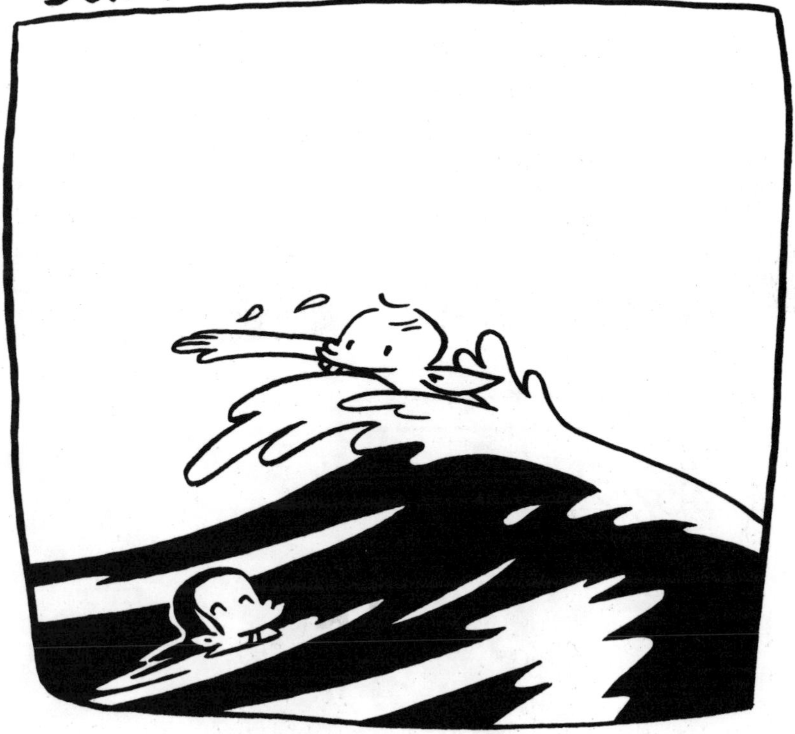

AMY WAS IN LABOR FOR ABOUT 20 HOURS. IT WAS A HEROIC STRUGGLE.

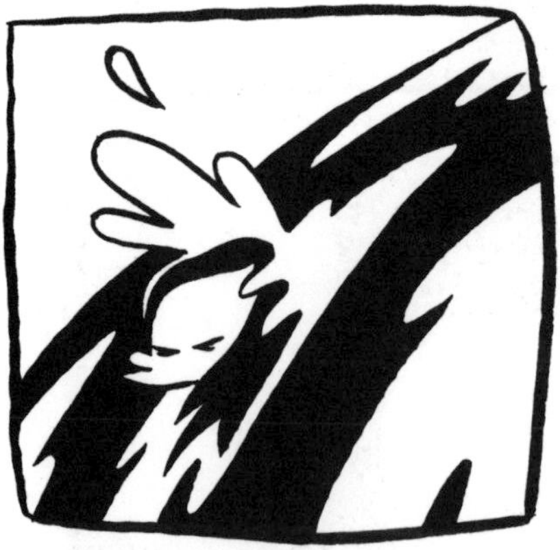

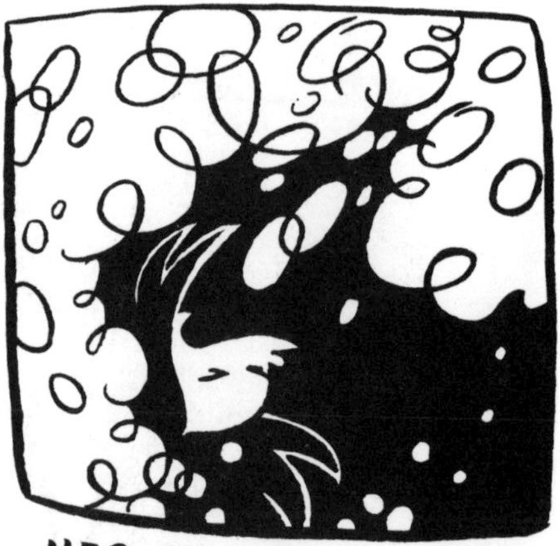

FIGHTING WITH ALL HER MIGHT TO HELP THAT BABY BOY BE BORN.

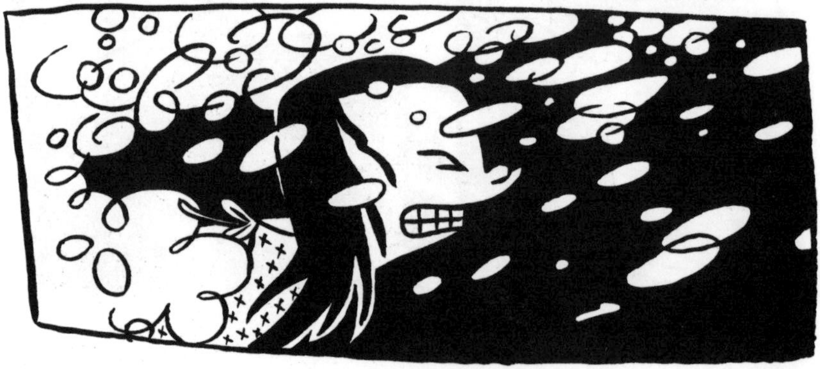

HOW SWEET & BEAUTIFUL SHE SEEMED WHILE RESTING BETWEEN CONTRACTIONS

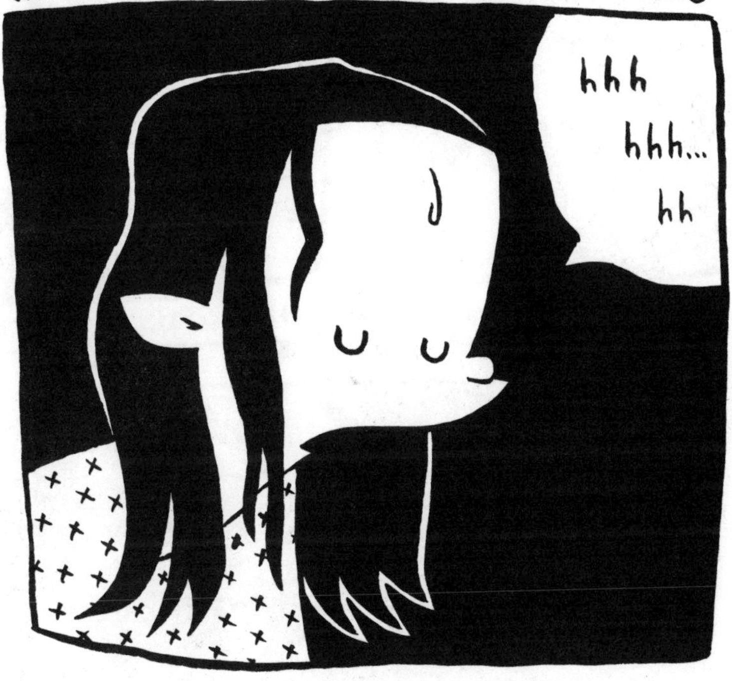
hhh
hhh...
hh

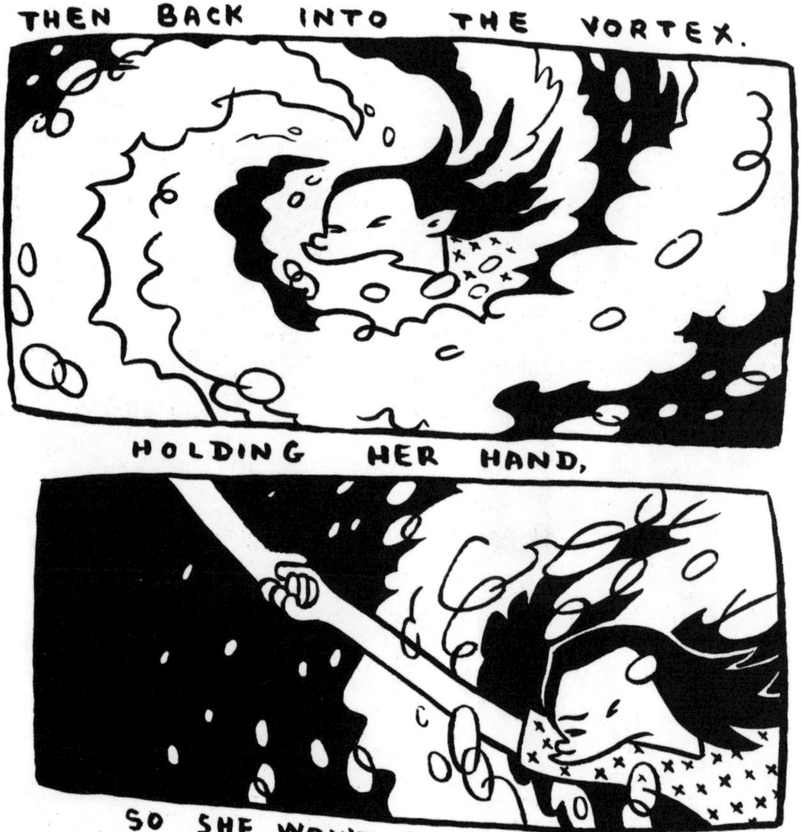
THEN BACK INTO THE VORTEX.
HOLDING HER HAND,
SO SHE WON'T BE SWEPT AWAY.

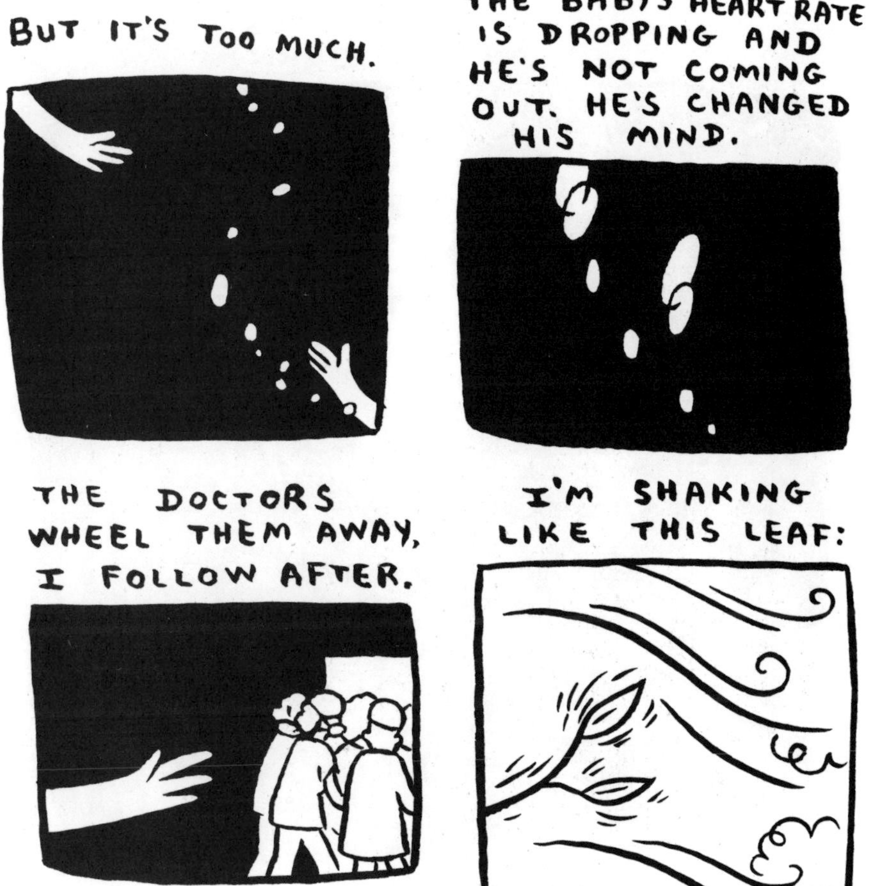
BUT IT'S TOO MUCH.
THE BABY'S HEARTRATE IS DROPPING AND HE'S NOT COMING OUT. HE'S CHANGED HIS MIND.
THE DOCTORS WHEEL THEM AWAY, I FOLLOW AFTER.
I'M SHAKING LIKE THIS LEAF:

THEY CUT HER OPEN AND OUR SON IS BORN.

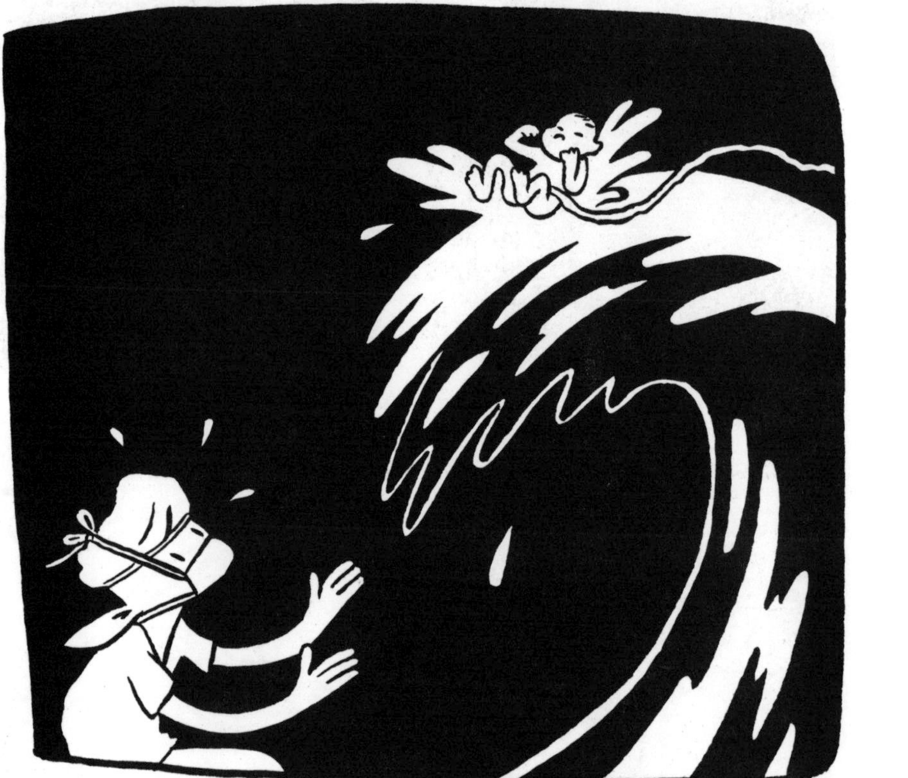

ELI RAY KOCHALKA

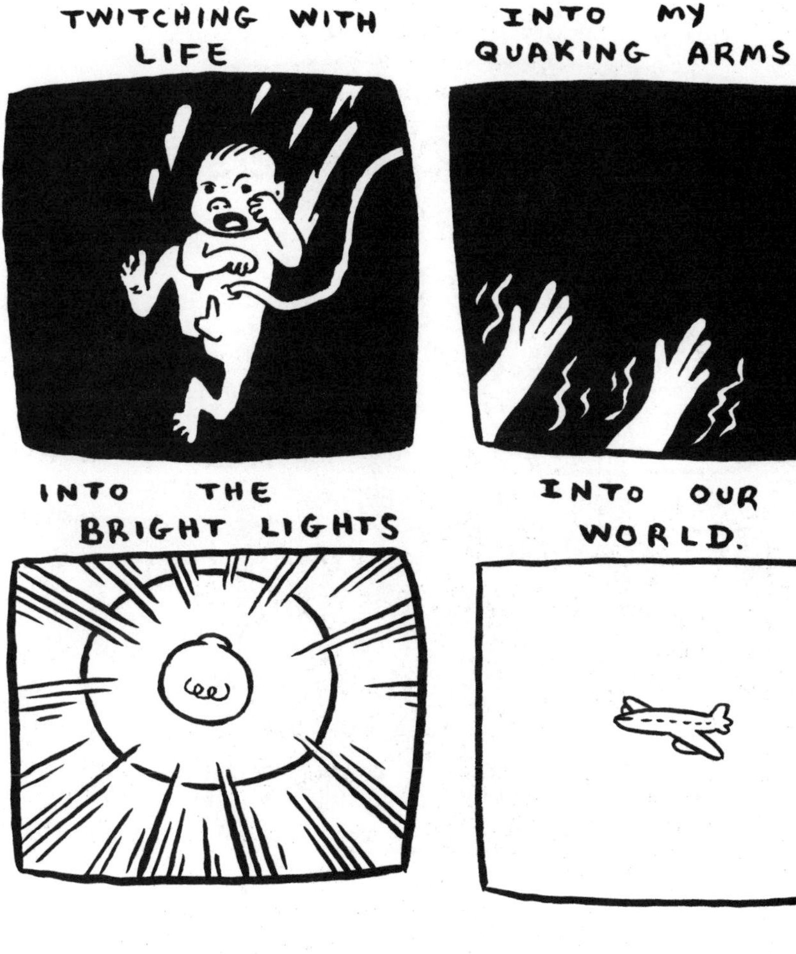
TWITCHING WITH LIFE
INTO MY QUAKING ARMS
INTO THE BRIGHT LIGHTS
INTO OUR WORLD.

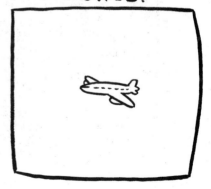

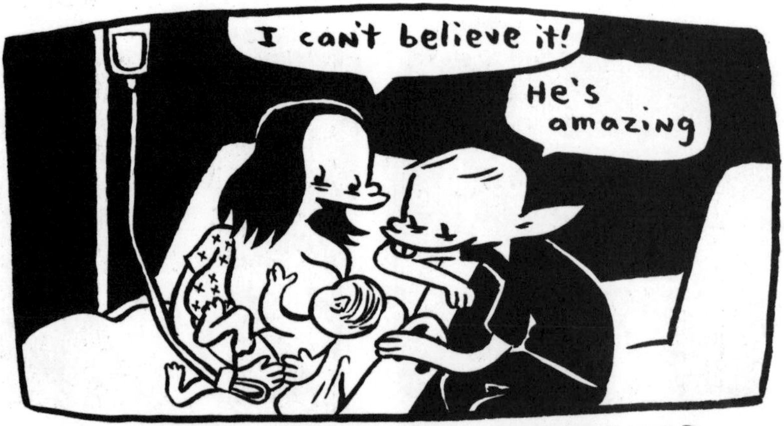
I can't believe it!
He's amazing

WE ALL SUCCUMB, EXHAUSTED,

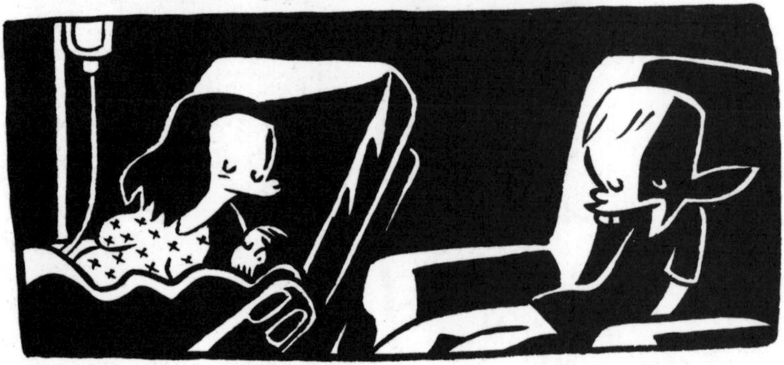

...DEEPLY TO THE NIGHT.

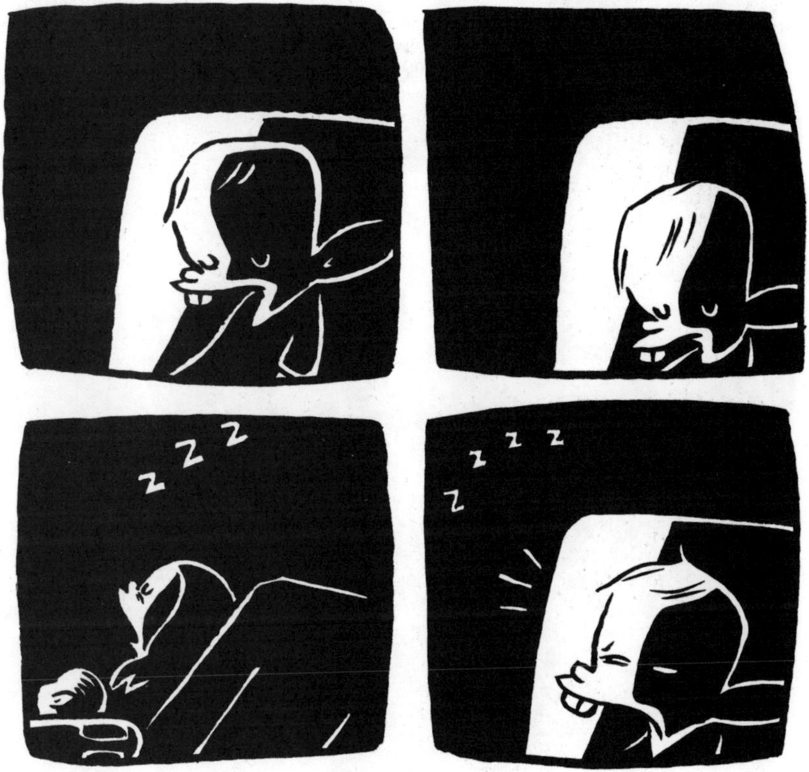
Z Z Z
Z Z Z Z

IN A BRIEF SEMI-CONSCIOUS STATE
I HAVE THE MOST HORRIBLE VISION
OF PINCHING MY SON'S LITTLE NOSE
AND SNUFFING OUT HIS NACSENT LIFE
IN AN ATTEMPT TO REVERSE
THE PROGRESSION OF TIME.

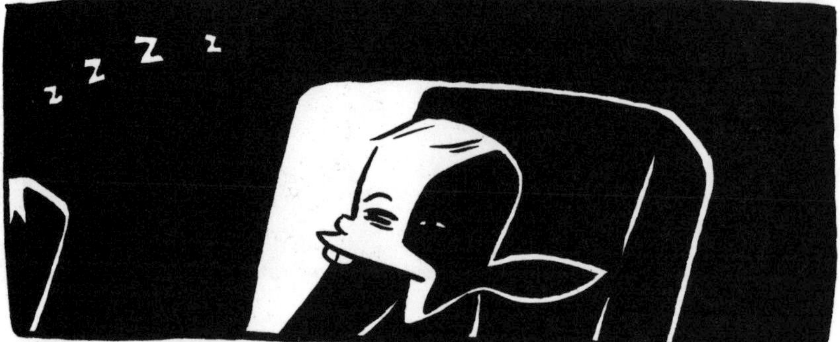
z z Z z

BUT THE THOUGHT FADES QUICKLY
AS I RE-SUBMERGE INTO THE
DEPTHS OF SLEEP.

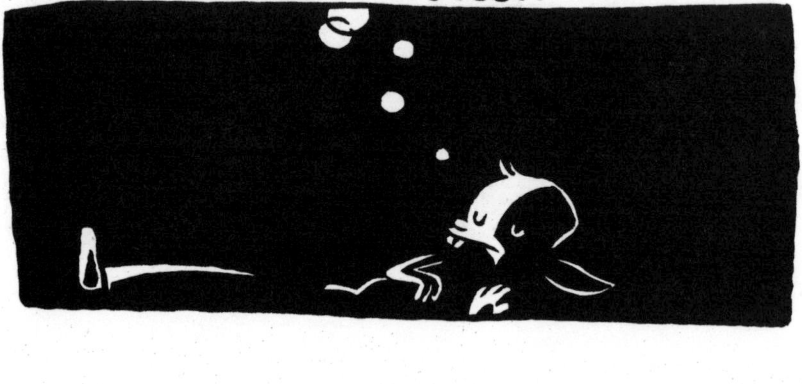

IN THE MORNING, I AWAKE TO A LIFE FULL OF BEAUTY & WONDER & LOVE. NEW HOUSE, NEW BABY, FRESH EYES.

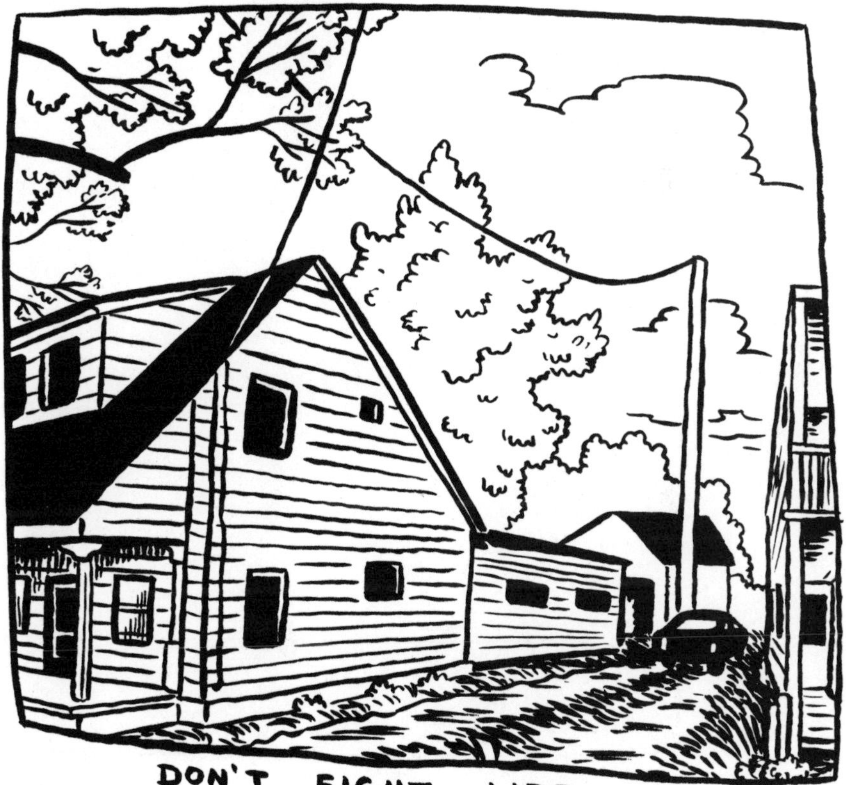

DON'T FIGHT LIFE.

THE CUTE

MANIFESTO

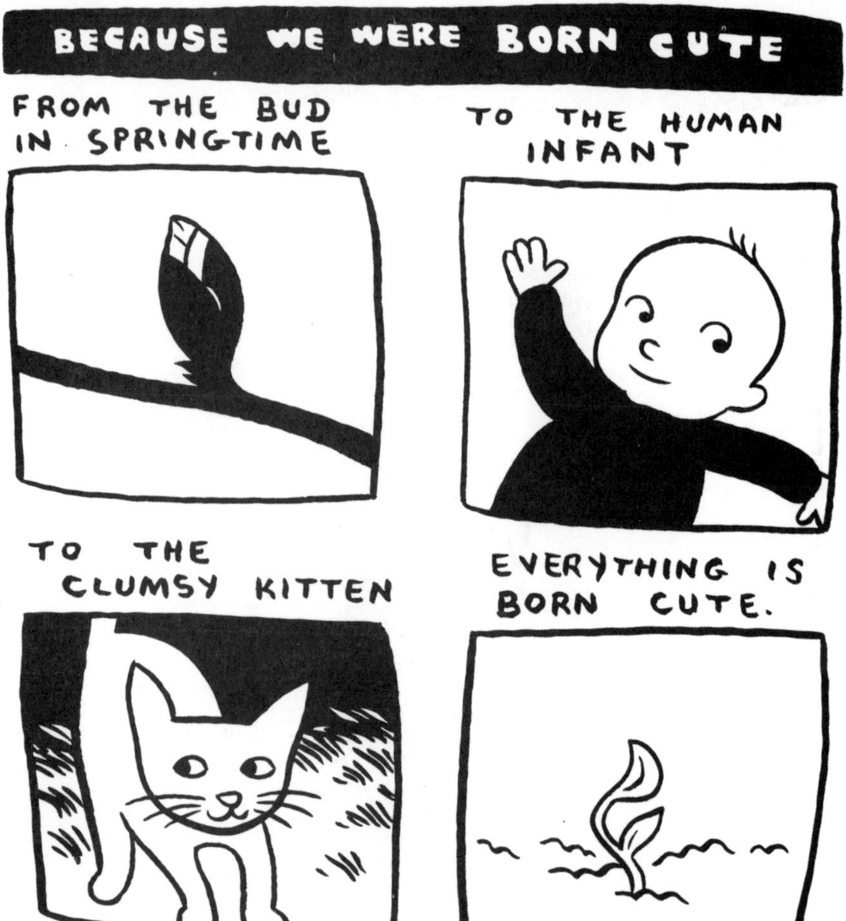
BECAUSE WE WERE BORN CUTE
FROM THE BUD IN SPRINGTIME
TO THE HUMAN INFANT
TO THE CLUMSY KITTEN
EVERYTHING IS BORN CUTE.

## BECAUSE CUTENESS IS PURE

ITS UNADULTERATED INNOCENCE SHINES LIKE A BEACON THROUGH THE DARKNESS OF THIS WORLD, UNTOUCHED BY EVIL OR GREED.

## BECAUSE IT IS STILL INSIDE US

SOME MAY SCOFF AND TRY TO DENY THE LEGITIMACY OF CUTE, BUT THEY THEMSELVES WERE SHINING EXAMPLES OF IT IN THEIR OWN INFANCY.

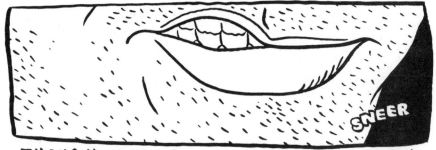

THOUGH OUR EXTERIORS MAY HARDEN AND GROW ROUGH, THE TWINKLE OF BEAUTY WITH WHICH WE WERE BORN REMAINS DEEP WITHIN US, FOREVER, AND IT SHINES THROUGH OUR TIRED EYES.

## BECAUSE CUTENESS WILL GROW

IF WE NURTURE THE CUTENESS WITHIN US, IT WILL GROW AND GROW

## BECAUSE WE LIVE FOR BEAUTY

THERE IS MUCH SUFFERING IN LIFE, BUT WE DO NOT EXIST MERELY TO SUFFER. WE EXIST TO FEEL JOY AND TO EXPERIENCE BEAUTY.

CUTENESS IS SIMPLY A PURE & RAREFIED FORM OF BEAUTY. NOTHING IS MORE BEAUTIFUL THAN THE CUTE BECAUSE THE CUTE IS UNTOUCHED BY ANY FOUL THOUGHT OR DEED.

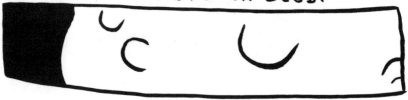

## BECAUSE THIS BEAUTY IS REAL

DESPITE THE SUFFERING AND DESTRUCTION THERE IS STILL JOY AND BEAUTY IN THIS WORLD SO PROFOUND THAT IT CANNOT BE DIMINISHED BY ANY UGLINESS OR EVIL.

ANYONE WHO HAS HELD THEIR BABY IN THEIR ARMS KNOWS THIS TO BE TRUE. IT IS MORE REAL THAN ANYTHING. ALL ELSE IS NOTHINGNESS.

## BECAUSE THE CHOICE IS CLEAR

EITHER WE TURN TOWARDS CUTENESS AND BEAUTY OR WE TURN TO FOLLOW SUFFERING AND DEATH.

SO WE TURN TOWARDS CUTENESS AND OPEN OUR HEARTS TO IT. ONLY ITS EXTREME PURITY CAN DELIVER US FROM UGLINESS AND SUFFERING.

FOR THESE REASONS WE CHOOSE CUTE.
WE DENY THE UGLINESS OF THE WORLD
AROUND US AND STAND IN OPPOSITION
TO IT. WHEN WE DRAW, OUR LINE
WILL BE AS SUPPLE AS THE PRECIOUS
SPRING TWIG AND AS RESILIENT AS
THE FAT CHEEKS OF AN INFANT. OUR
ART SHALL REMAIN AS PURE AND
INNOCENT AS THE SLEEPING BABE AND
IT SHALL SHINE WITH THE INQUISITIVE
TWINKLE OF HIS WIDE, WAKING EYES. WE
SHALL NOT USE CUTENESS TO CHAMPION
CRASS COMMERCIAL VENTURES, FOR THAT USE
MERELY SERVES TO CORRUPT AND DEFILE,
TWISTING CUTENESS FROM BEAUTY INTO
UGLINESS. NOR DO WE LIVE IN A FANTASY
WORLD WHERE WE PRETEND THAT SUFFERING
DOES NOT OCCUR. RATHER, WE FIGHT
FOR BEAUTY AND PURITY AND WE FIGHT TO
MAKE THE WORLD A MORE JOYFUL PLACE.
THIS IS THE CUTE MANIFESTO.

# THE HORRIBLE TRUTH ABOUT COMICS

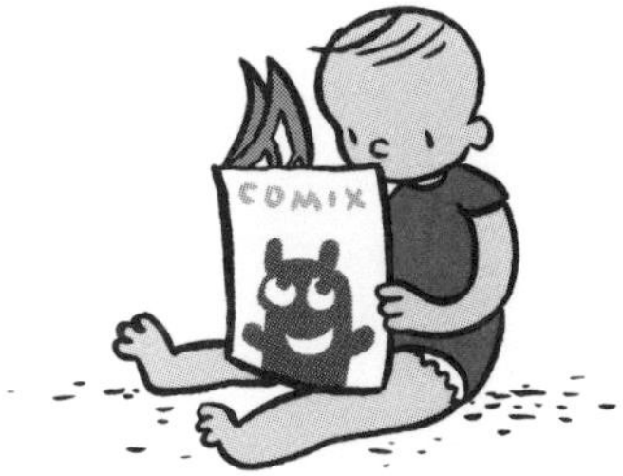
COMIX

stop
wiggling

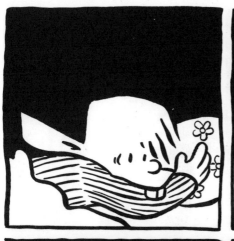

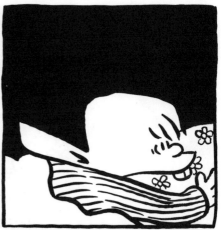

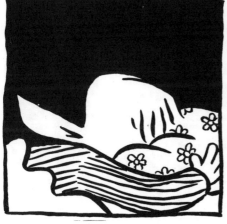

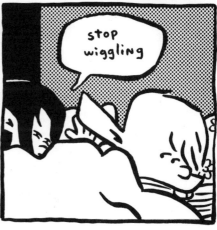

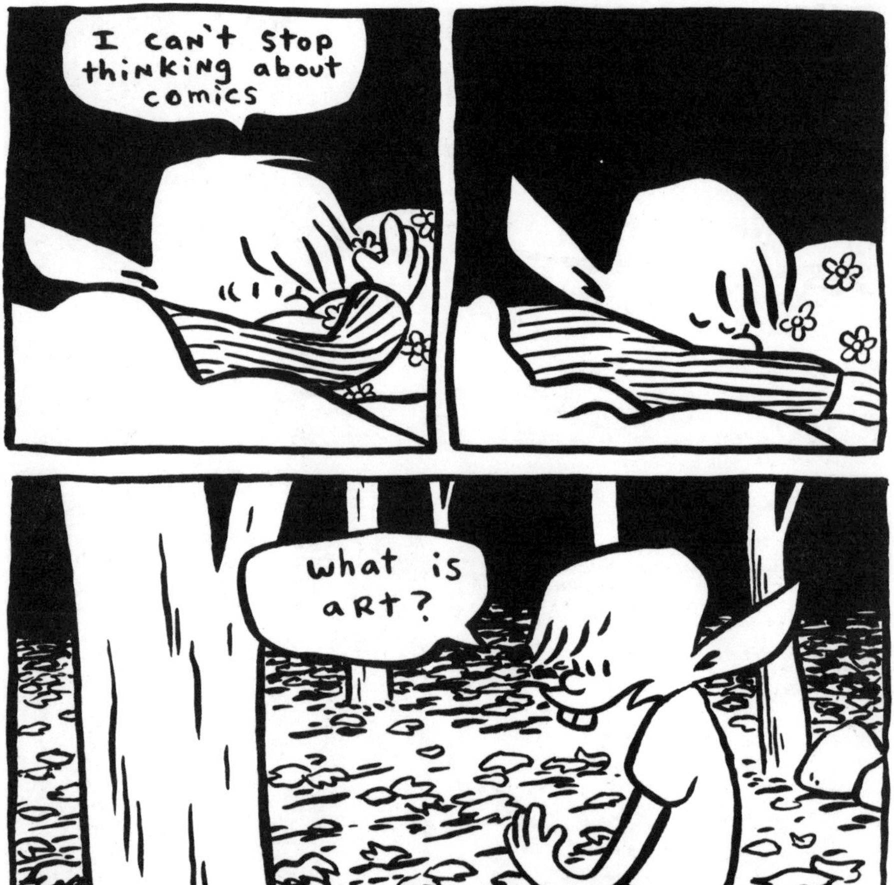
I can't stop thinking about comics
what is art?

Art is one of our most basic means for understanding the world around us. We process what we've experienced and recreate it in simplified form

Often this brings revelations that we could not come by through sheer reason

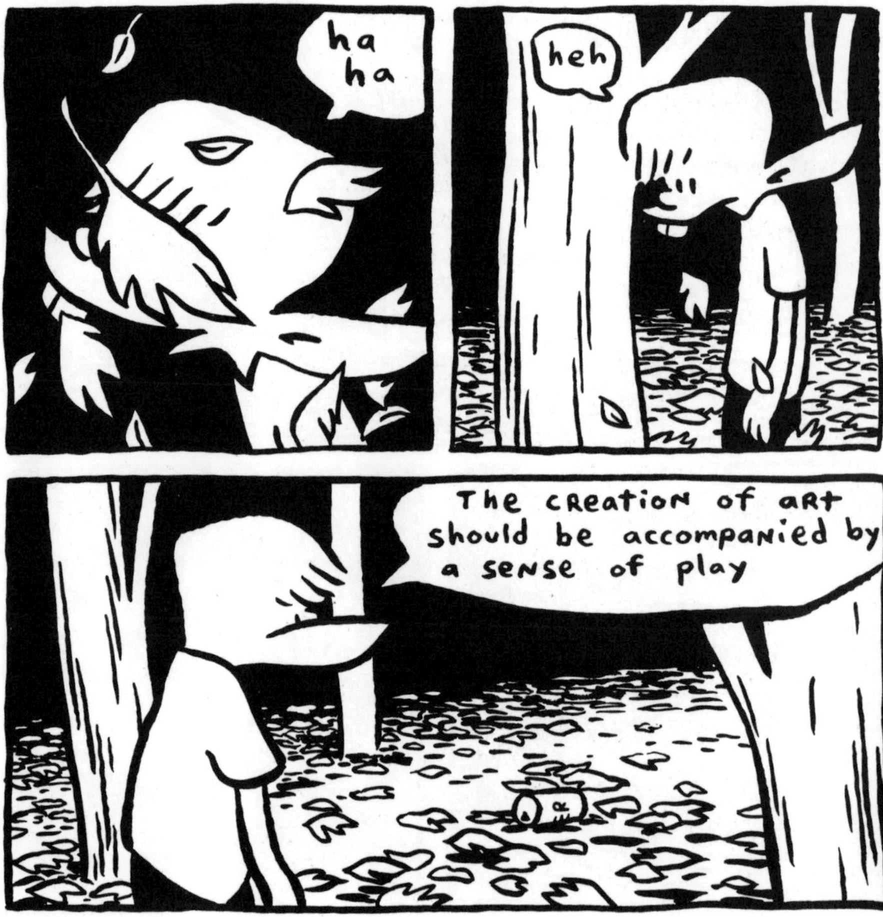
ha ha
heh
The creation of art should be accompanied by a sense of play

take that
BEE
KLANK
ER
play is a heightened state of imaginative awareness that allows us to enter new Realms of discovery

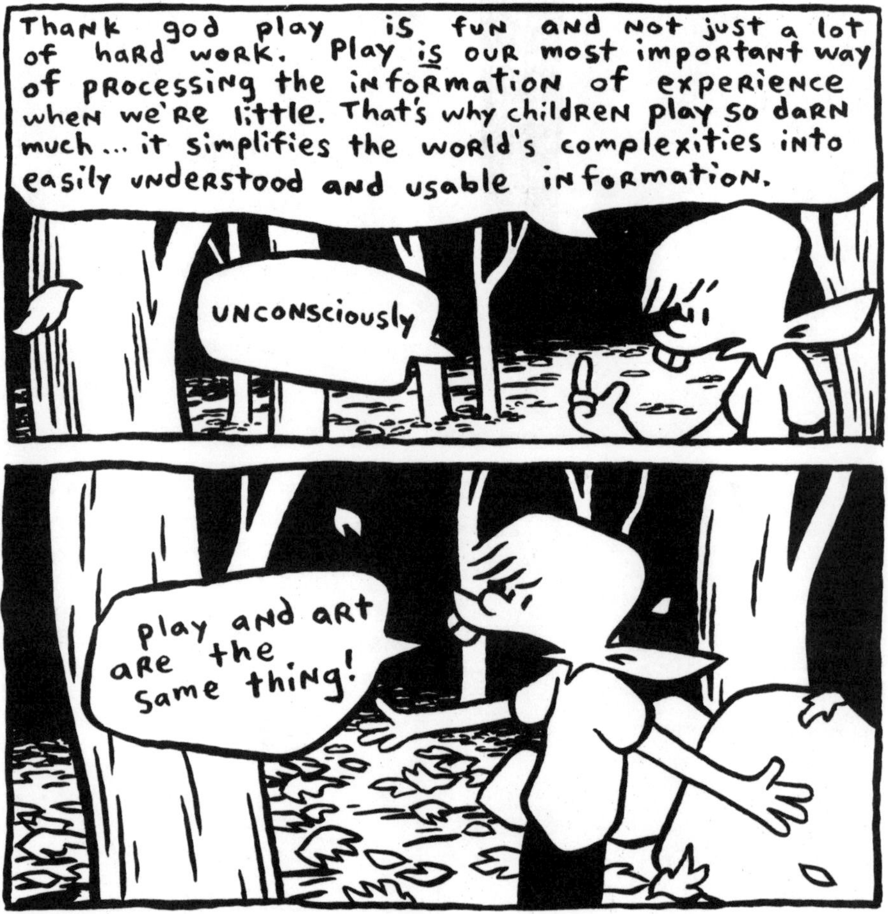
Thank god play is fun and not just a lot of hard work. Play is our most important way of processing the information of experience when we're little. That's why children play so darn much... it simplifies the world's complexities into easily understood and usable information.
unconsciously
play and art are the same thing!

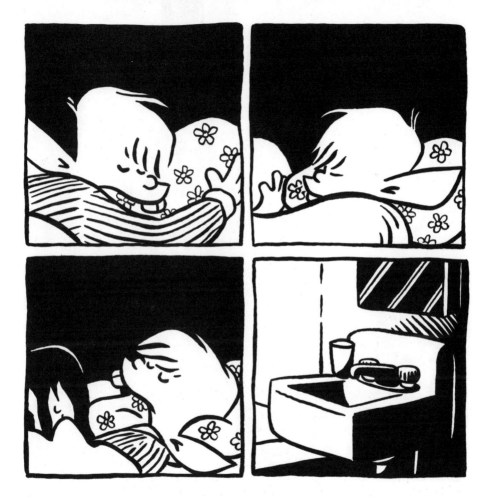

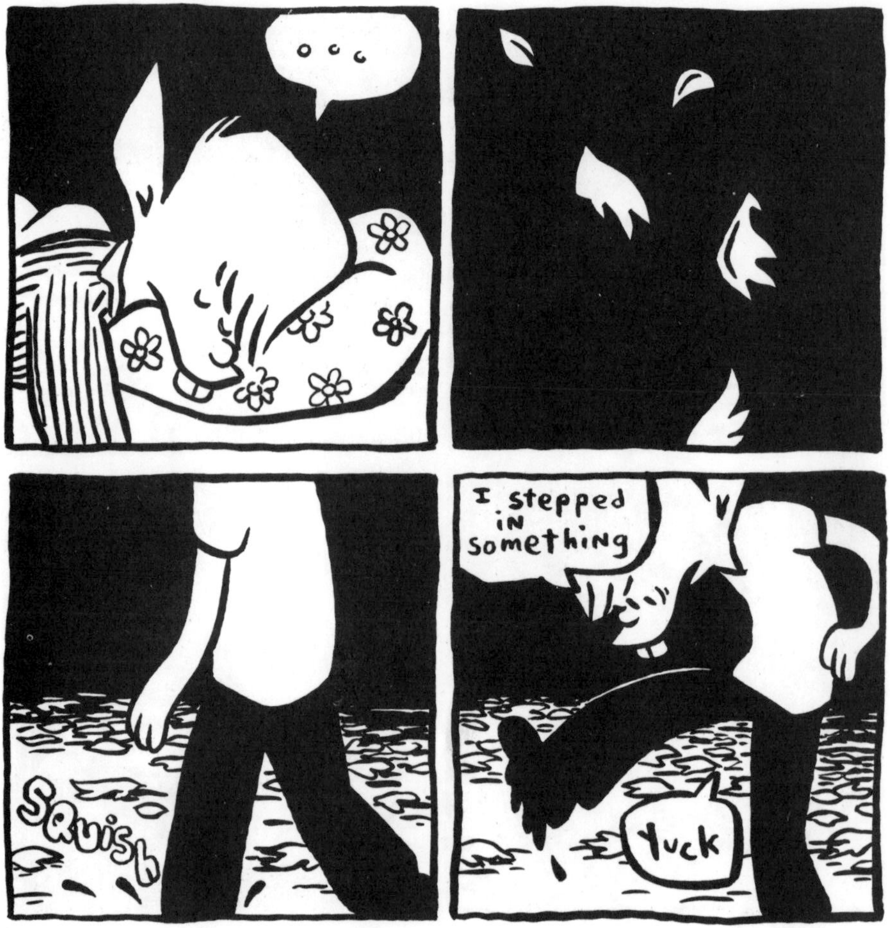
...
SQUISH
I stepped in something
yuck

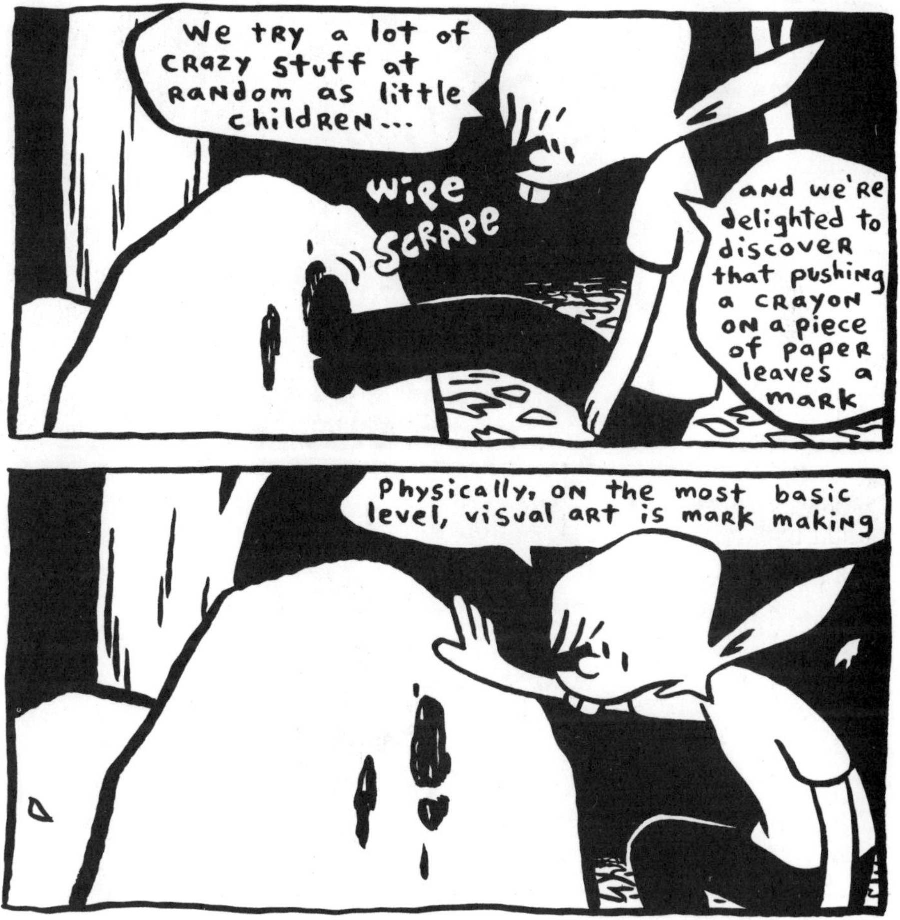
We try a lot of crazy stuff at random as little children...
wipe
scrape
and we're delighted to discover that pushing a crayon on a piece of paper leaves a mark
Physically, on the most basic level, visual art is mark making

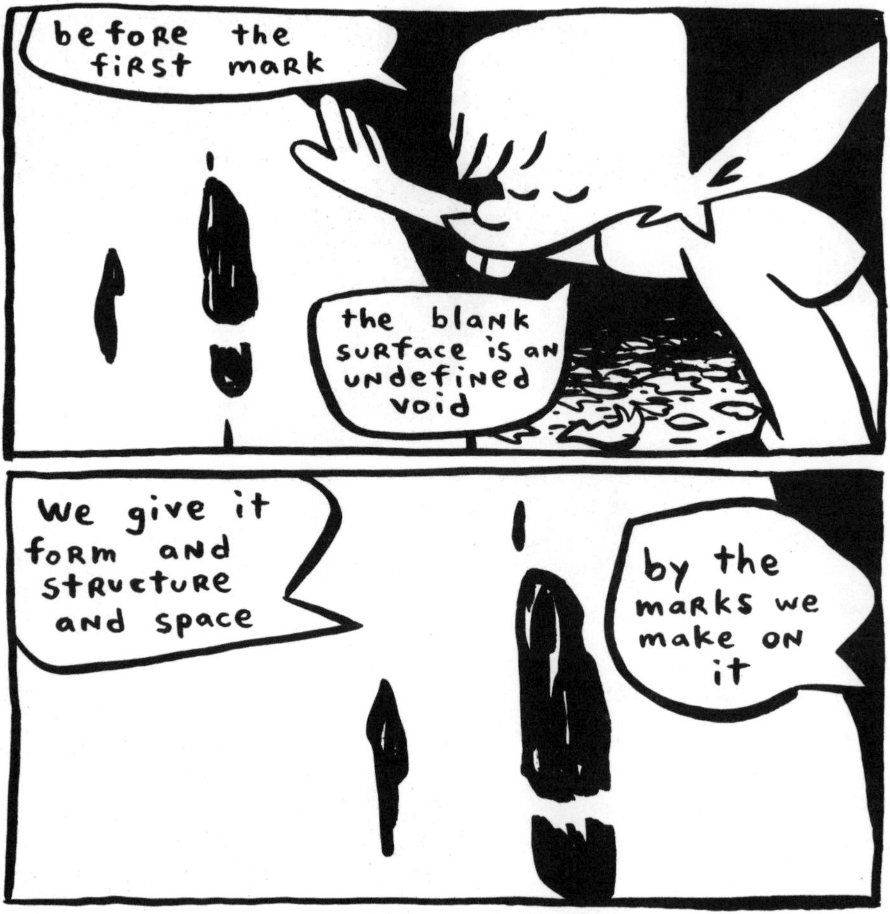
before the first mark
the blank surface is an undefined void
we give it form and structure and space
by the marks we make on it

this happens accidentally at first
then we learn to structure the space consciously
Perhaps a wild scribble
to chop the void up into definable chunks

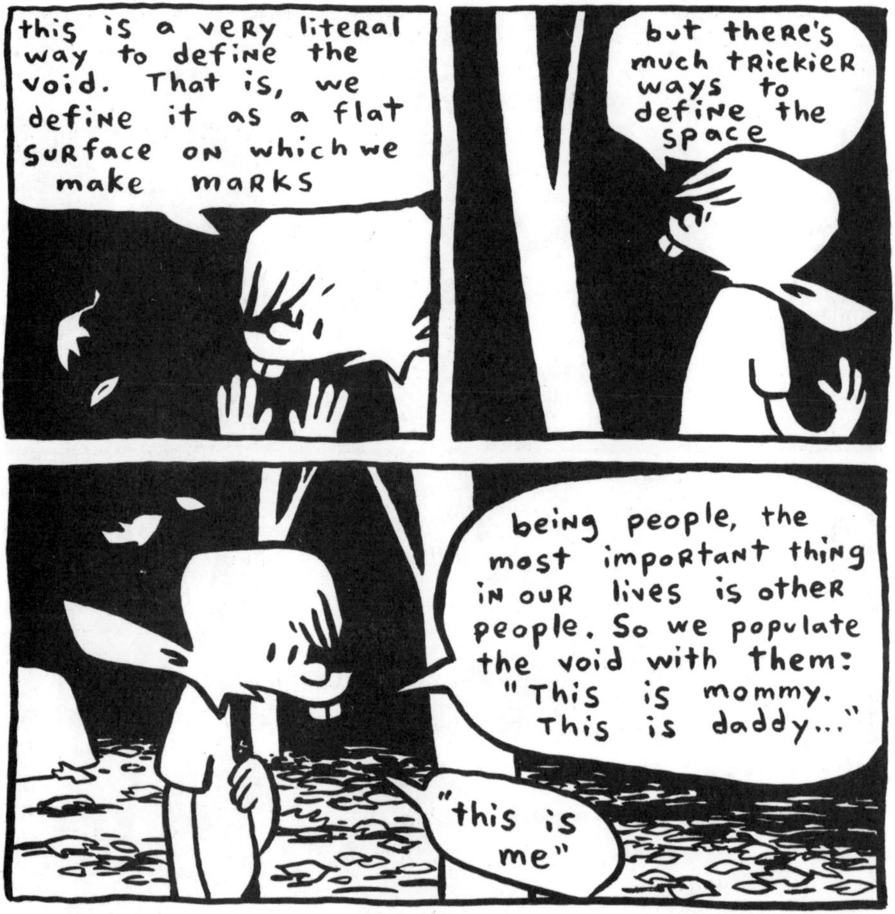
this is a very literal way to define the void. That is, we define it as a flat surface on which we make marks
but there's much trickier ways to define the space
being people, the most important thing in our lives is other people. So we populate the void with them: "This is mommy. This is daddy..."
"this is me"

We create a New world within the void
a simplification of the world we live in
every child is God, creating his own universe

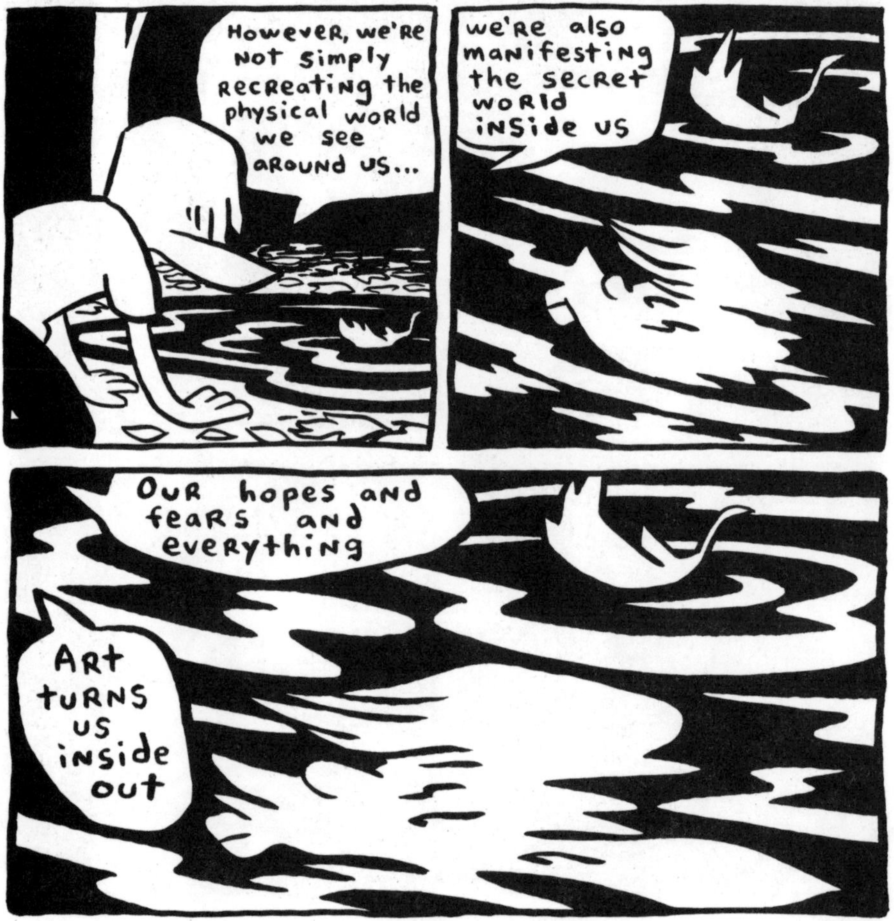
However, we're not simply recreating the physical world we see around us...
we're also manifesting the secret world inside us
Our hopes and fears and everything
Art turns us inside out

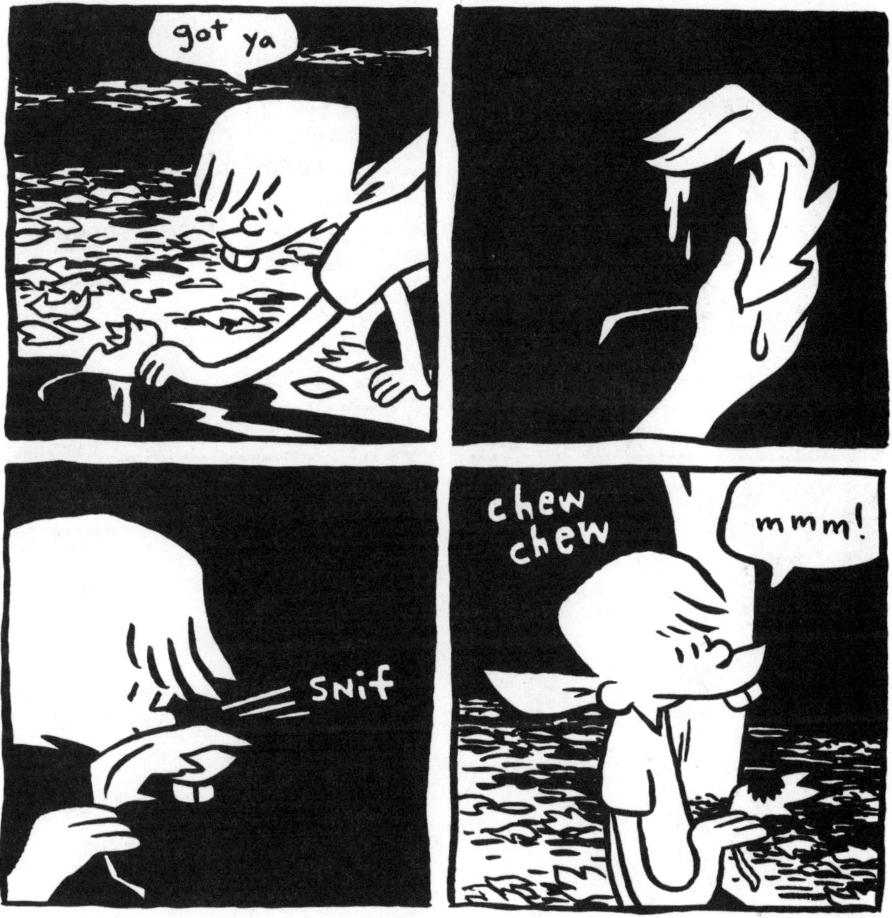
got ya
SNif
chew chew
mmm!

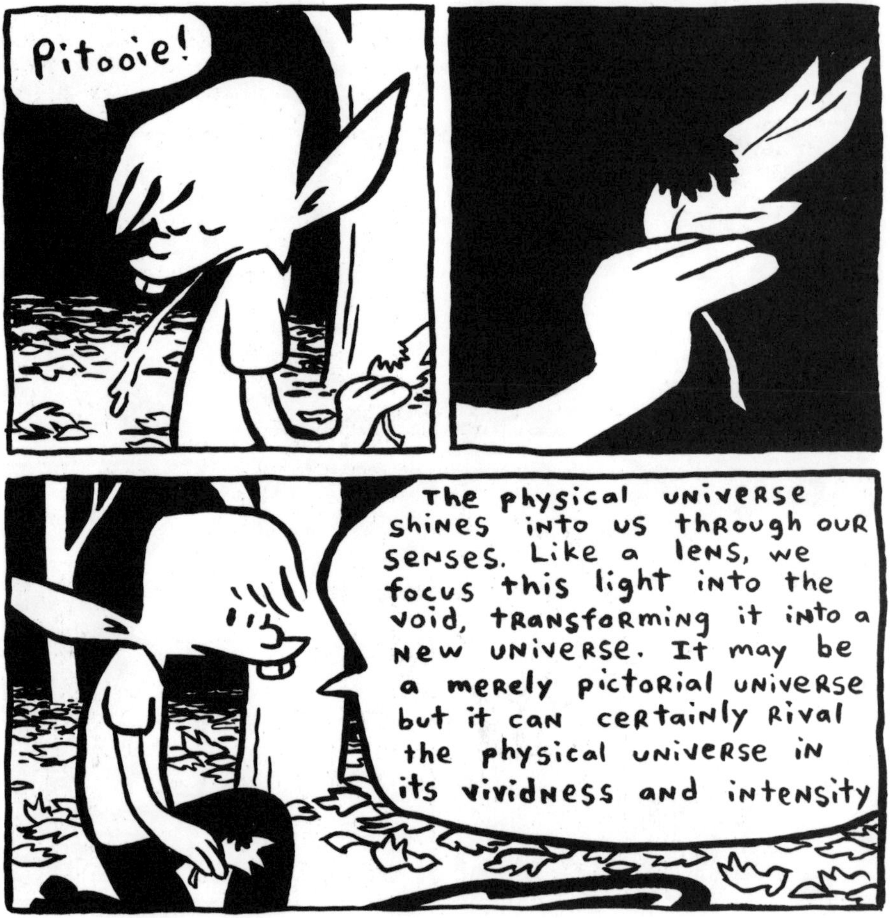
Pitooie!
The physical universe shines into us through our senses. Like a lens, we focus this light into the void, transforming it into a new universe. It may be a merely pictorial universe but it can certainly rival the physical universe in its vividness and intensity

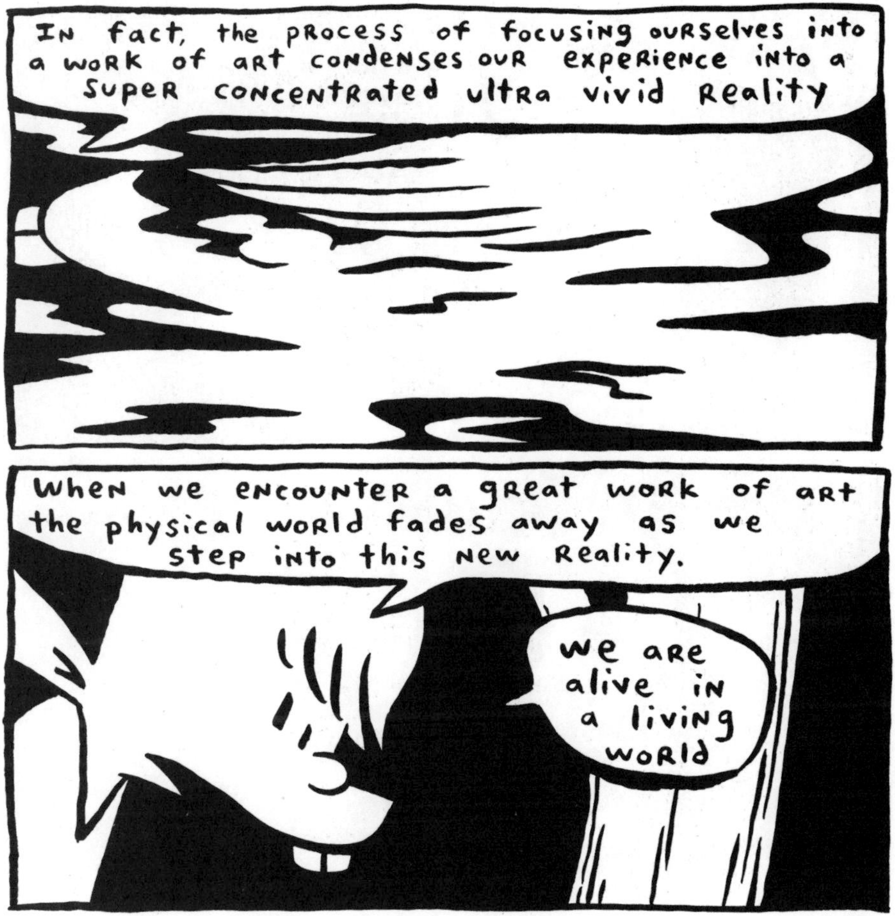

In fact, the process of focusing ourselves into a work of art condenses our experience into a super concentrated ultra vivid Reality
When we encounter a great work of art the physical world fades away as we step into this new Reality.
we are alive in a living world

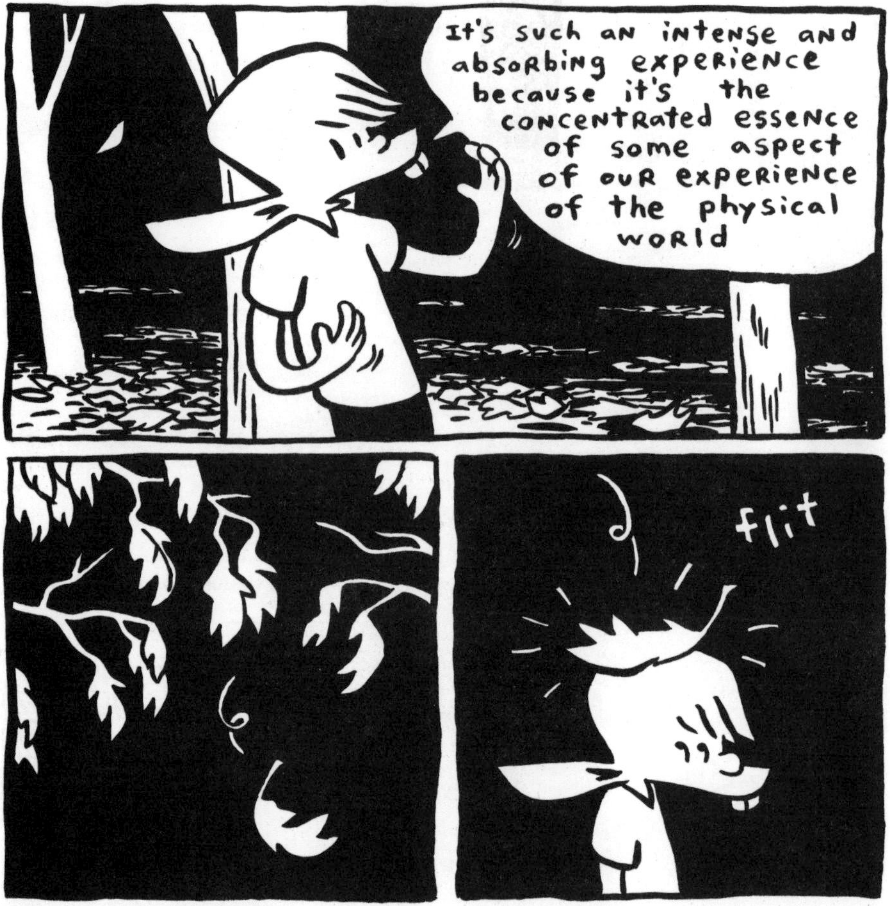
It's such an intense and absorbing experience because it's the concentrated essence of some aspect of our experience of the physical world
flit

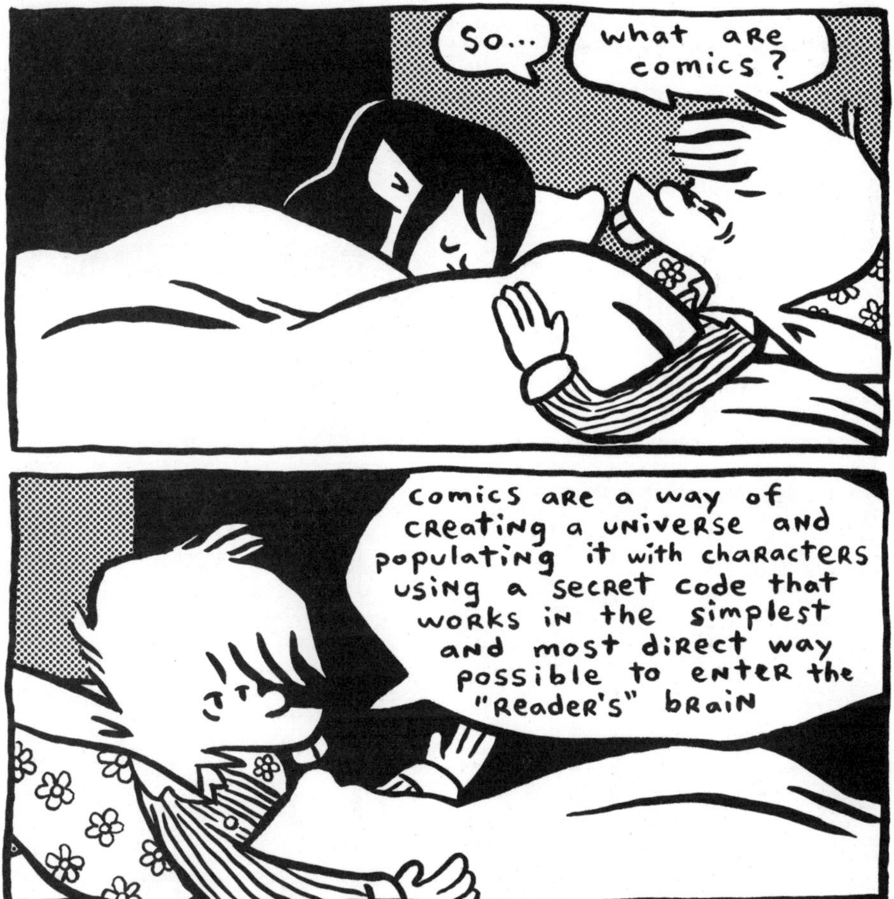

So...
what are comics?
comics are a way of creating a universe and populating it with characters using a secret code that works in the simplest and most direct way possible to enter the "reader's" brain

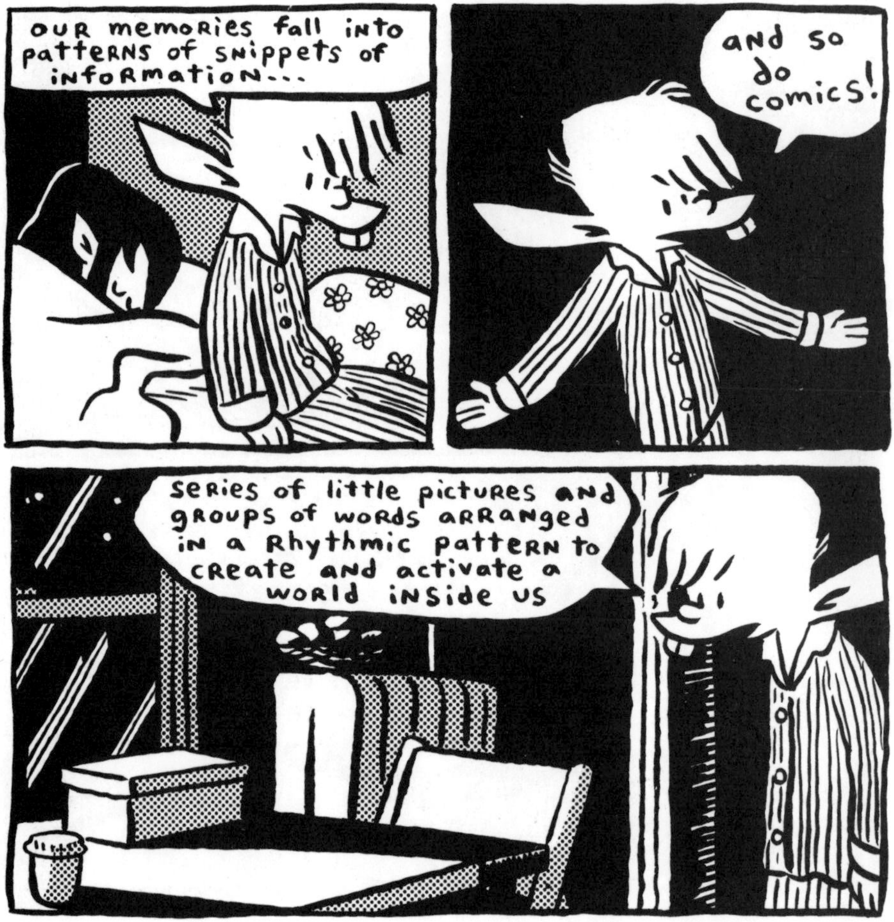
our memories fall into patterns of snippets of information...
and so do comics!
series of little pictures and groups of words arranged in a rhythmic pattern to create and activate a world inside us

gulp!

The structure of comics matches the pattern of wiring in our brains. This is why they offer such a direct line to our inner being

Melody is the most important part of music. Melody is the meaning of music, the part that touches us and makes our heart sing. But without Rhythm to carry it along, melody falls apart

Rhythm is what delivers melody into the brain

In comics, melody and Rhythm come together in the continuing transitions from panel to panel

Our brains long for our experiences to fall into understandable patterns and rhythms. Comics offer this in abundance...
Rhythm is the key...
...
So...

...what is art NOT?
well, as I've described it, Art is not about communication

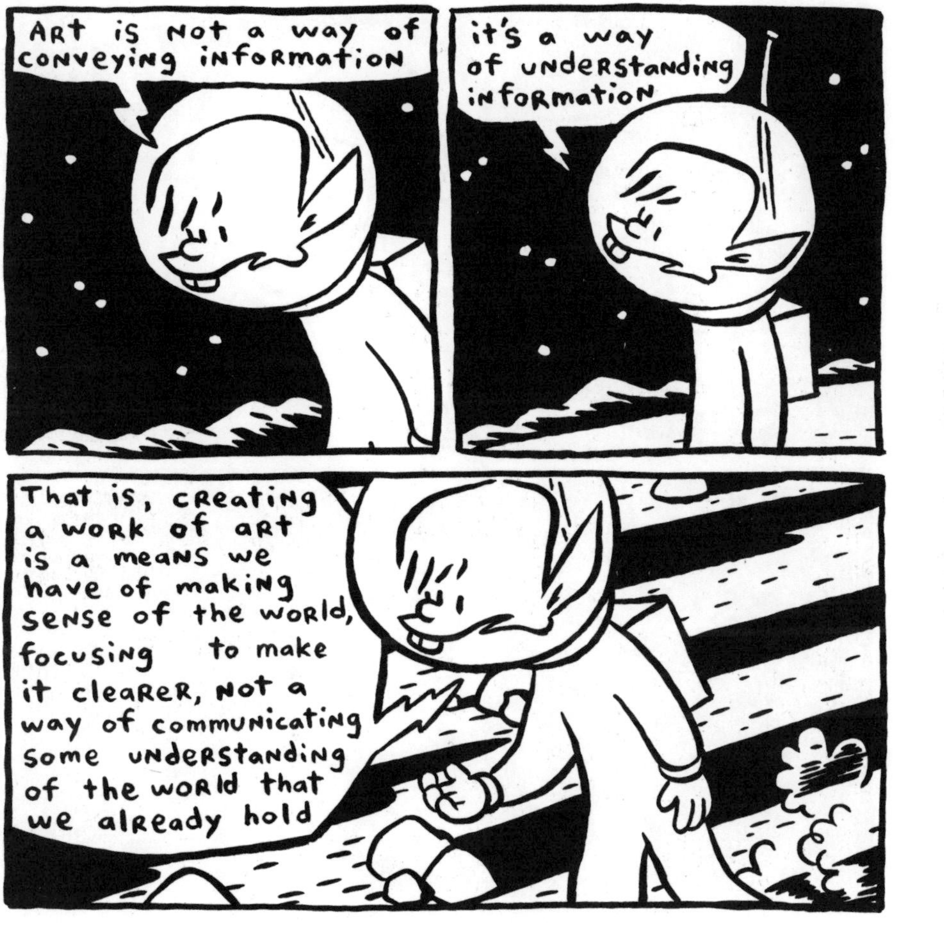
ART is NOT a way of conveying information
it's a way of understanding information
That is, creating a work of art is a means we have of making sense of the world, focusing to make it clearer, not a way of communicating some understanding of the world that we already hold

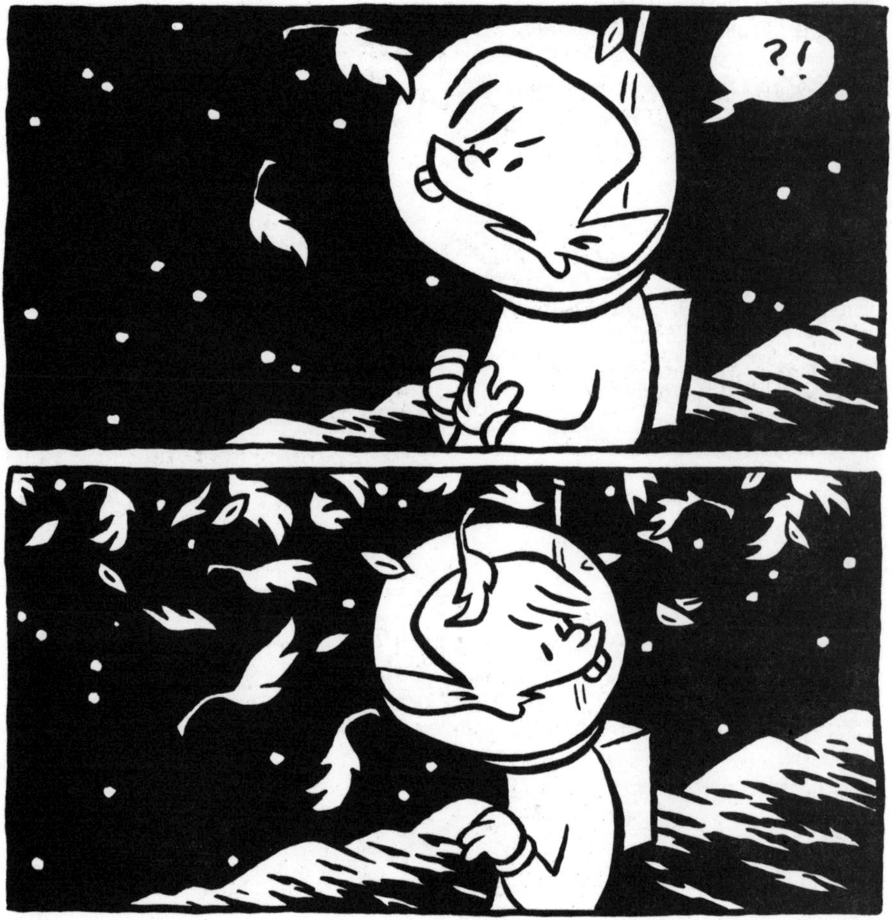
?!

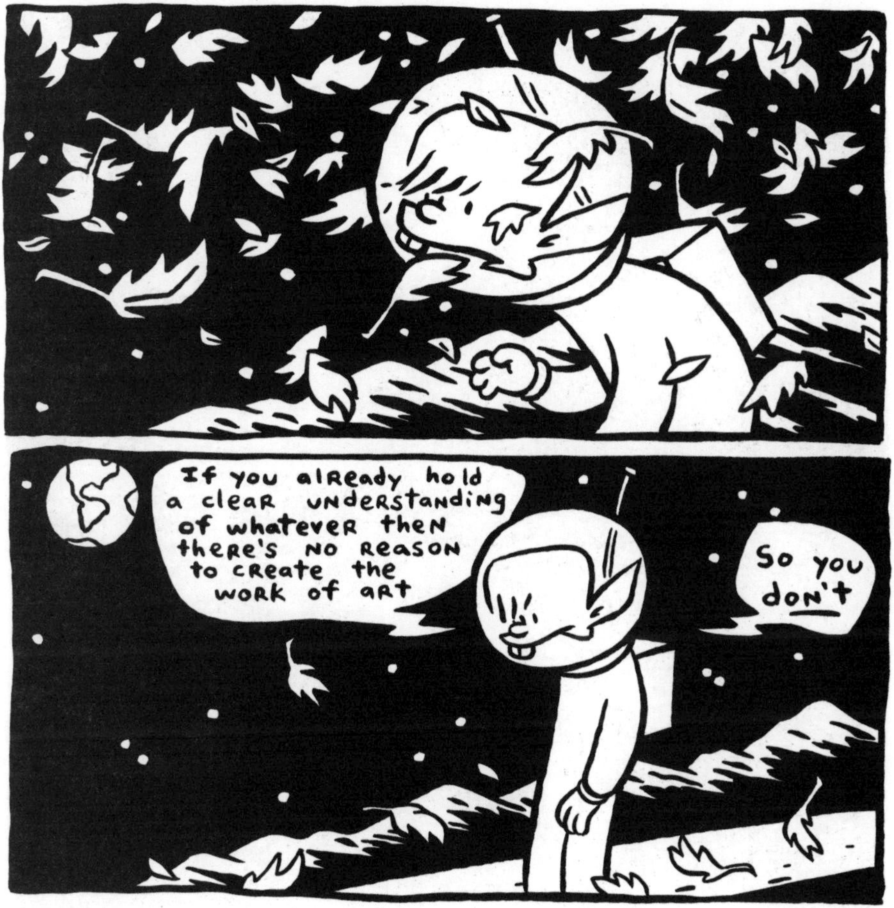
If you already hold a clear understanding of whatever then there's no reason to create the work of art
So you don't

IN fact, you can't

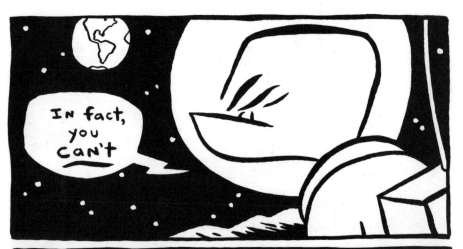

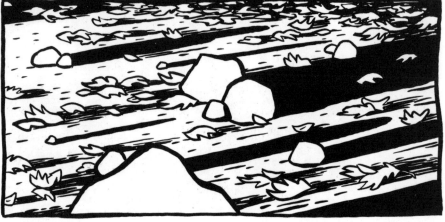

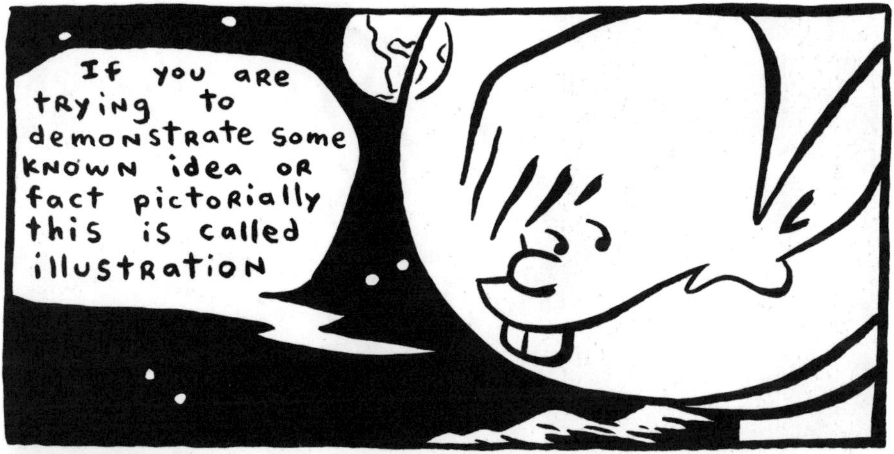
If you are trying to demonstrate some known idea or fact pictorially this is called illustration

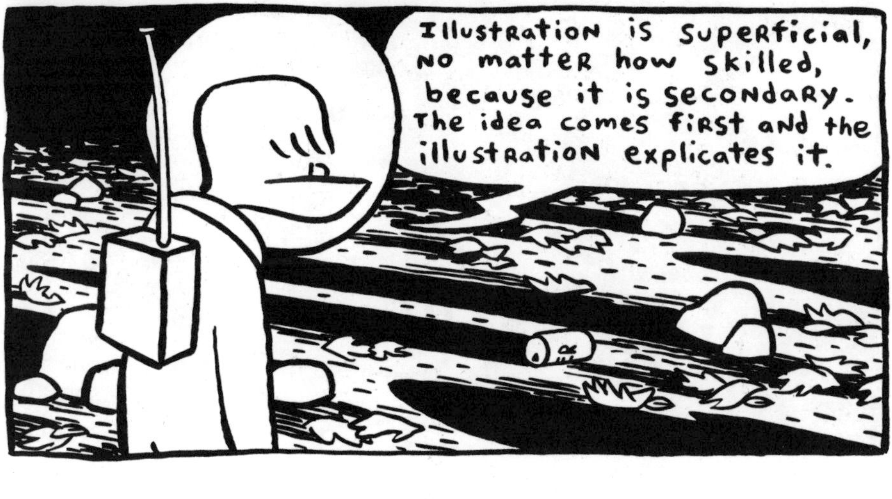
Illustration is superficial, no matter how skilled, because it is secondary. The idea comes first and the illustration explicates it.

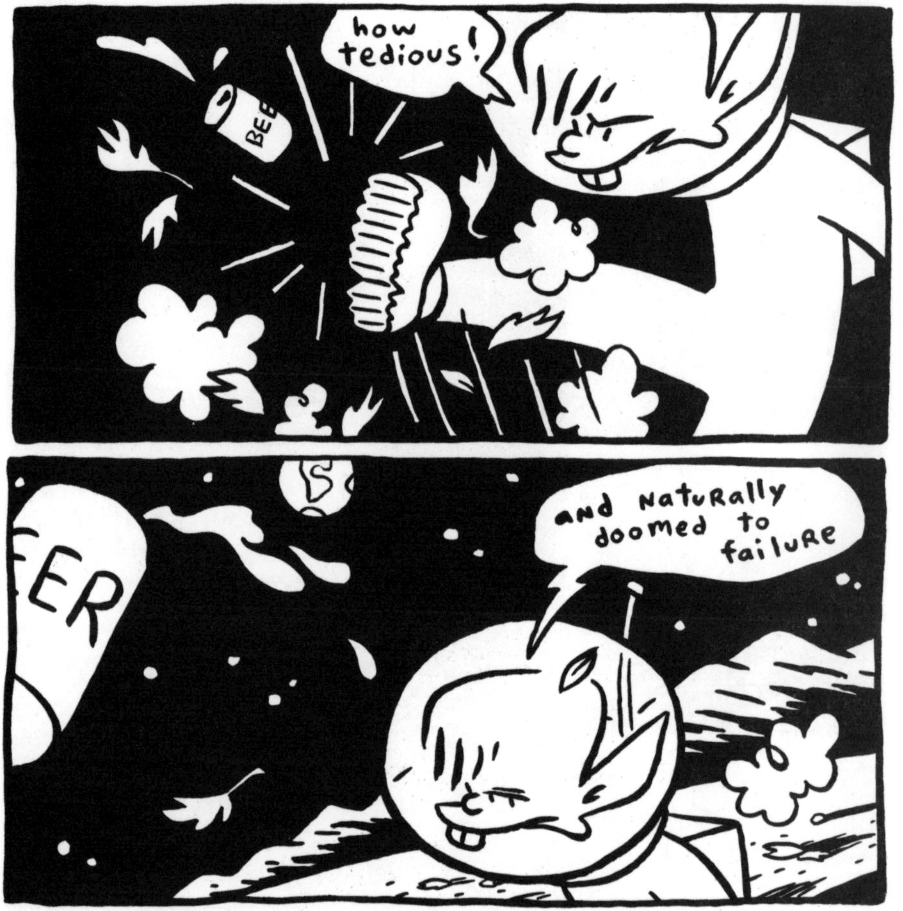
how tedious!
BEE
and NatuRally doomed to failuRe
ER

It's importantant to make a determination on the notion of "quality"

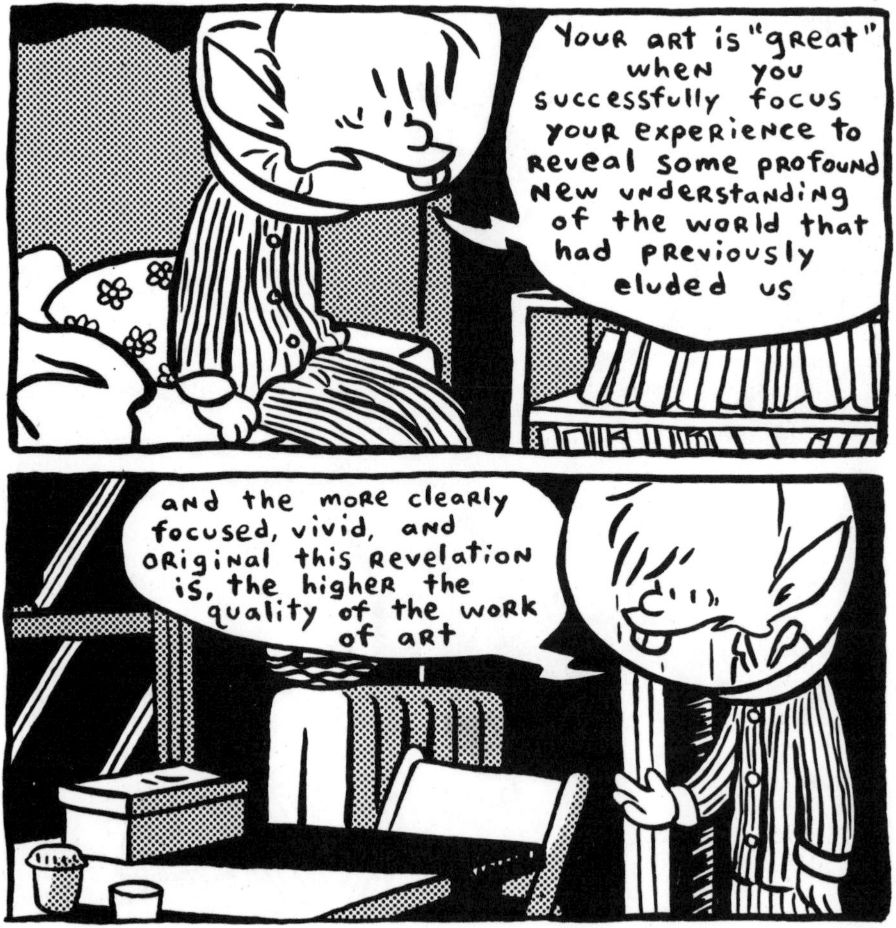
Your art is "great" when you successfully focus your experience to reveal some profound new understanding of the world that had previously eluded us
and the more clearly focused, vivid, and original this revelation is, the higher the quality of the work of art

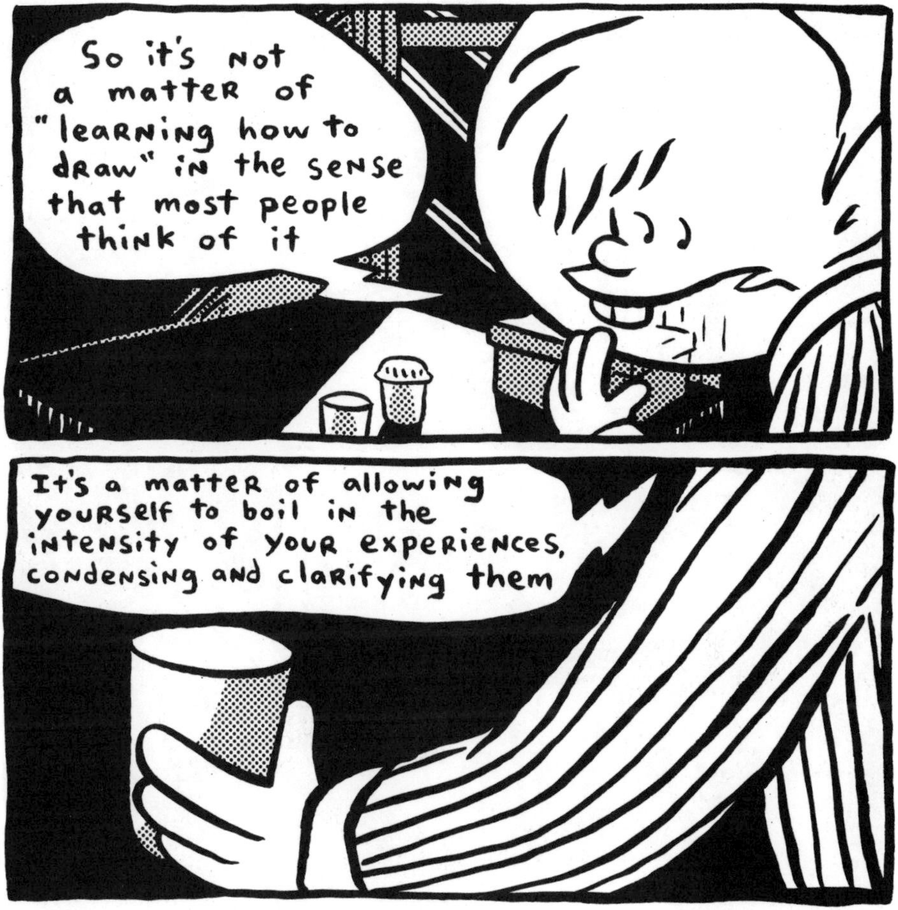
So it's not a matter of "learning how to draw" in the sense that most people think of it
It's a matter of allowing yourself to boil in the intensity of your experiences, condensing and clarifying them

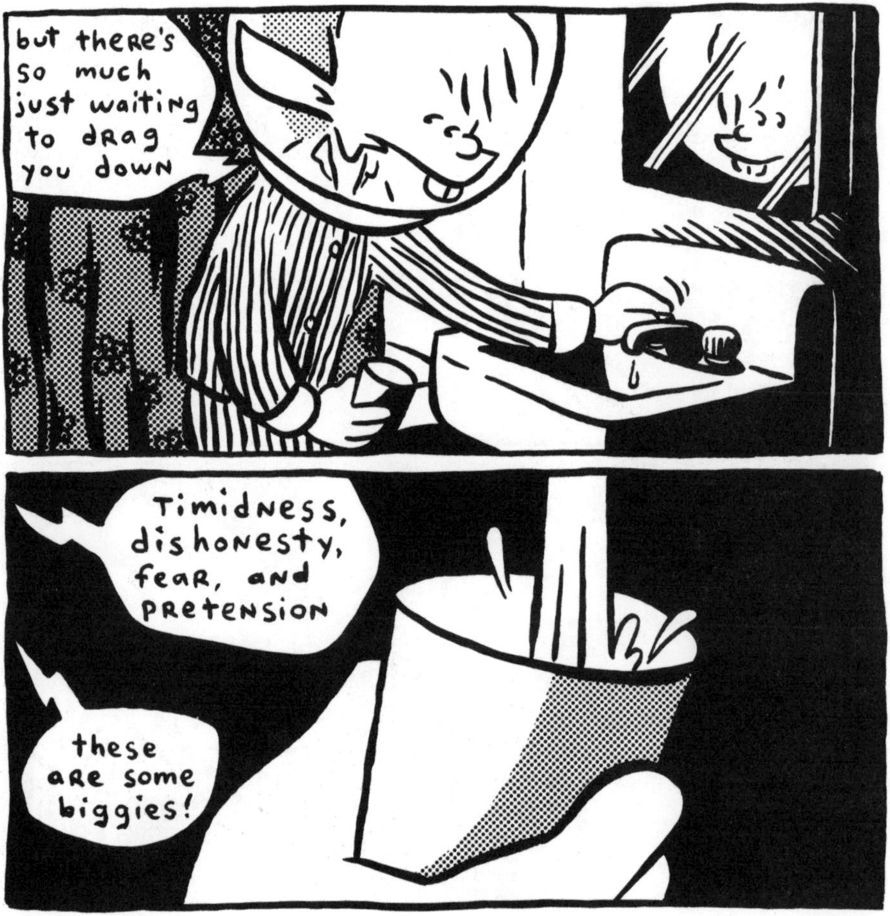
but there's so much just waiting to drag you down
Timidness, dishonesty, fear, and pretension
these are some biggies!

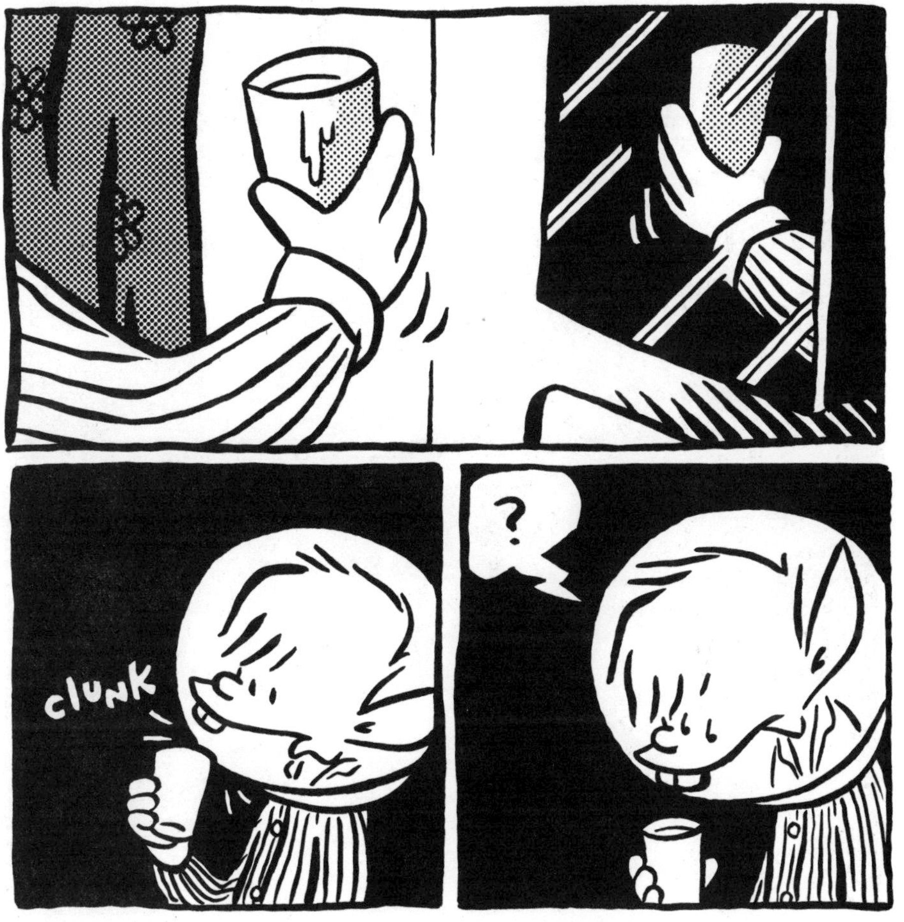
CLUNK
?

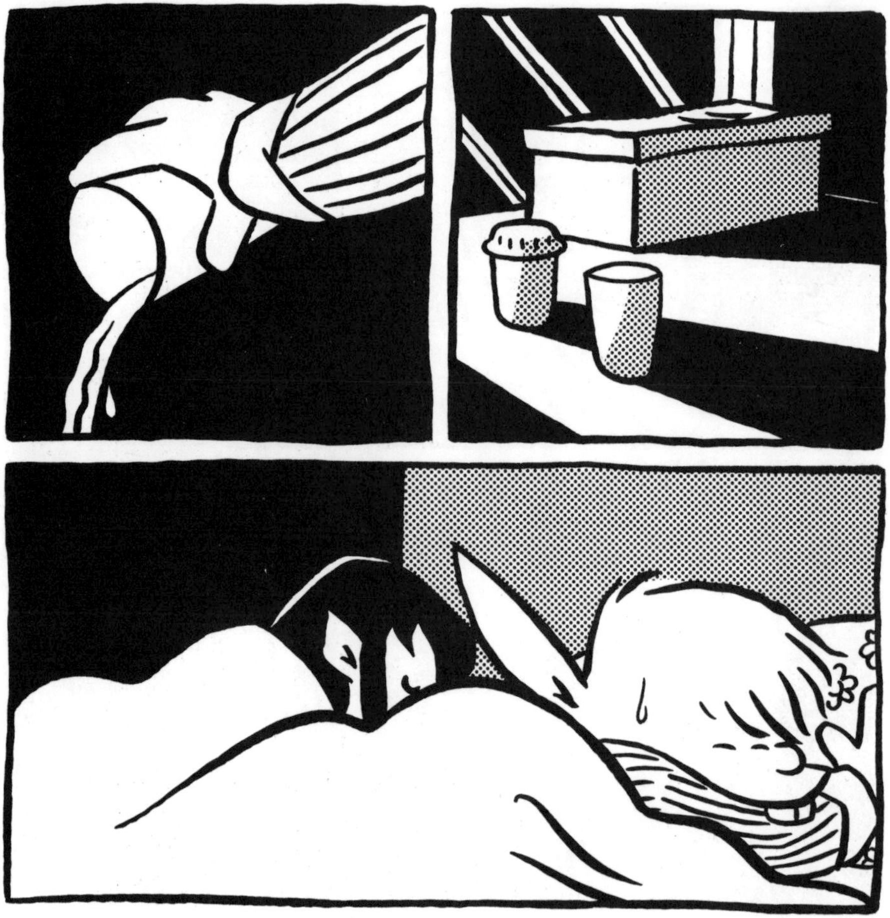

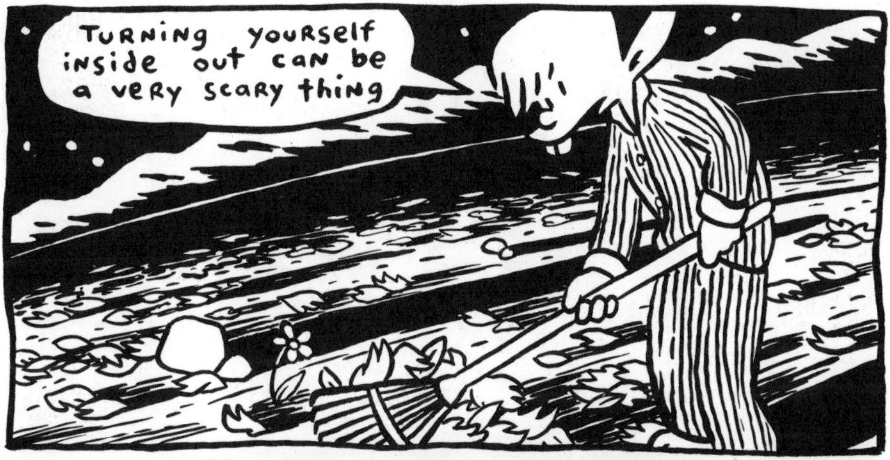
TURNING yourself inside out can be a very scary thing

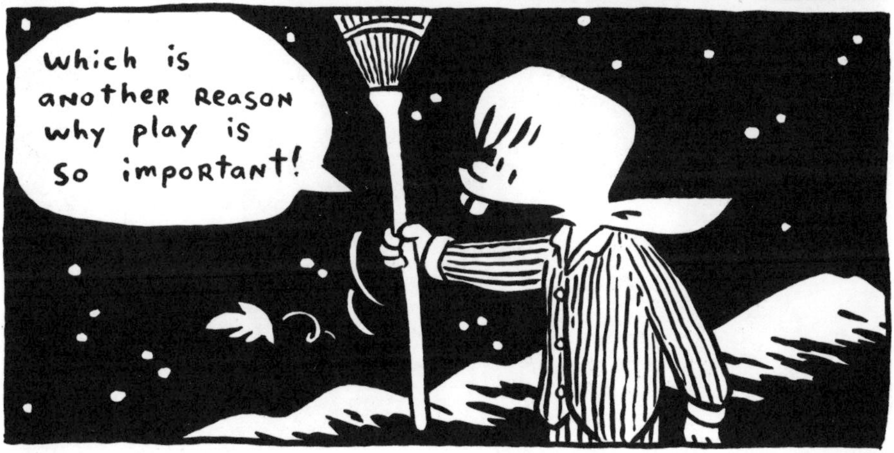
which is another reason why play is so important!

It allows you to reveal yourself in a disarmingly joyful manner

Soon you'll find you've struck upon a great truth dug out of the deep recesses of your soul...

...as easily as plucking a petal from a daisy

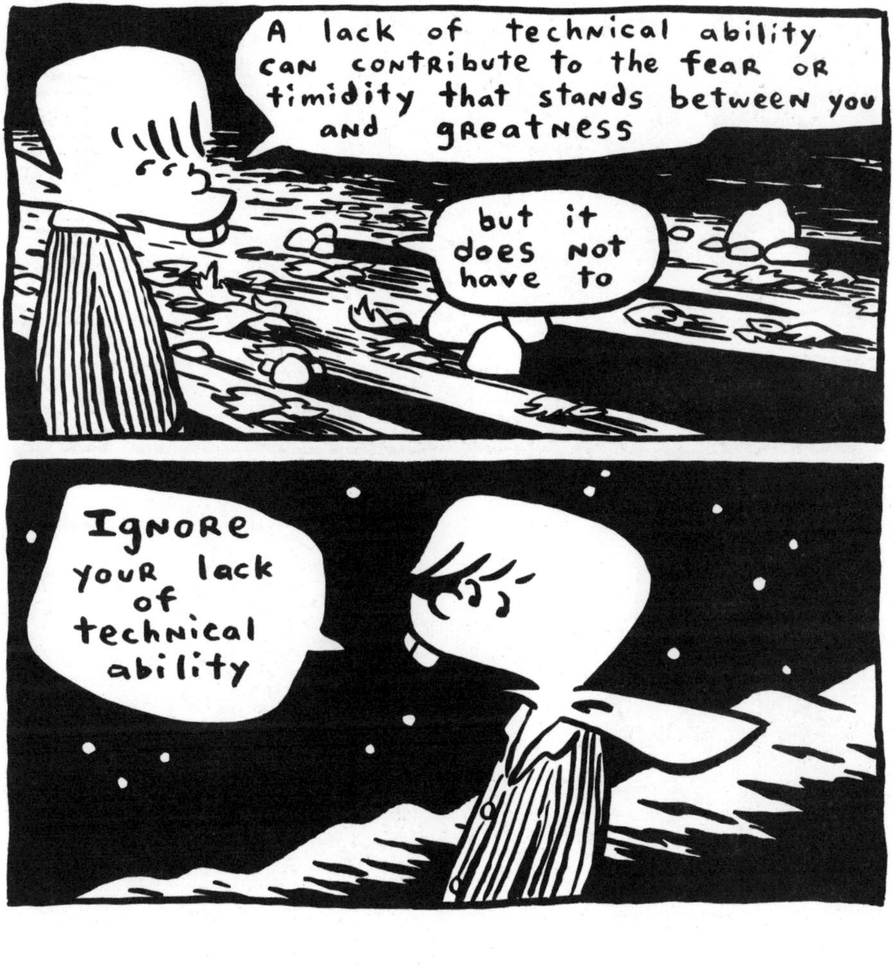
A lack of technical ability can contribute to the fear or timidity that stands between you and greatness
but it does not have to
Ignore your lack of technical ability

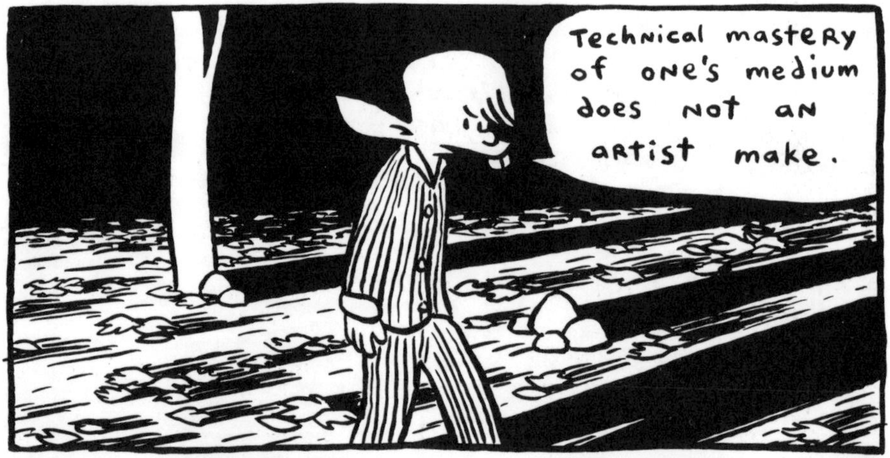
Technical mastery of one's medium does not an artist make.

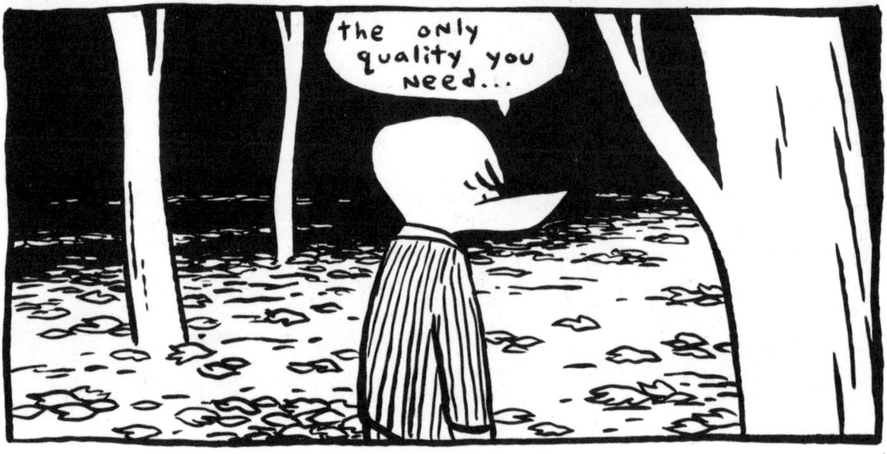
the only quality you need...

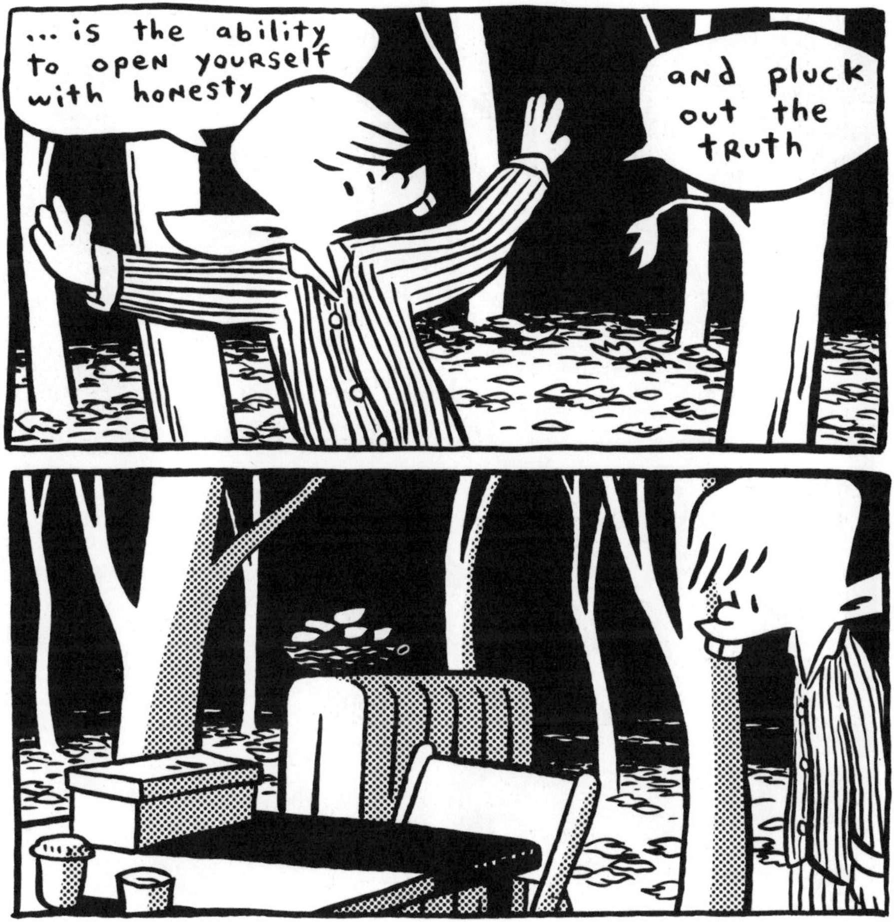
... is the ability to open yourself with honesty
and pluck out the truth

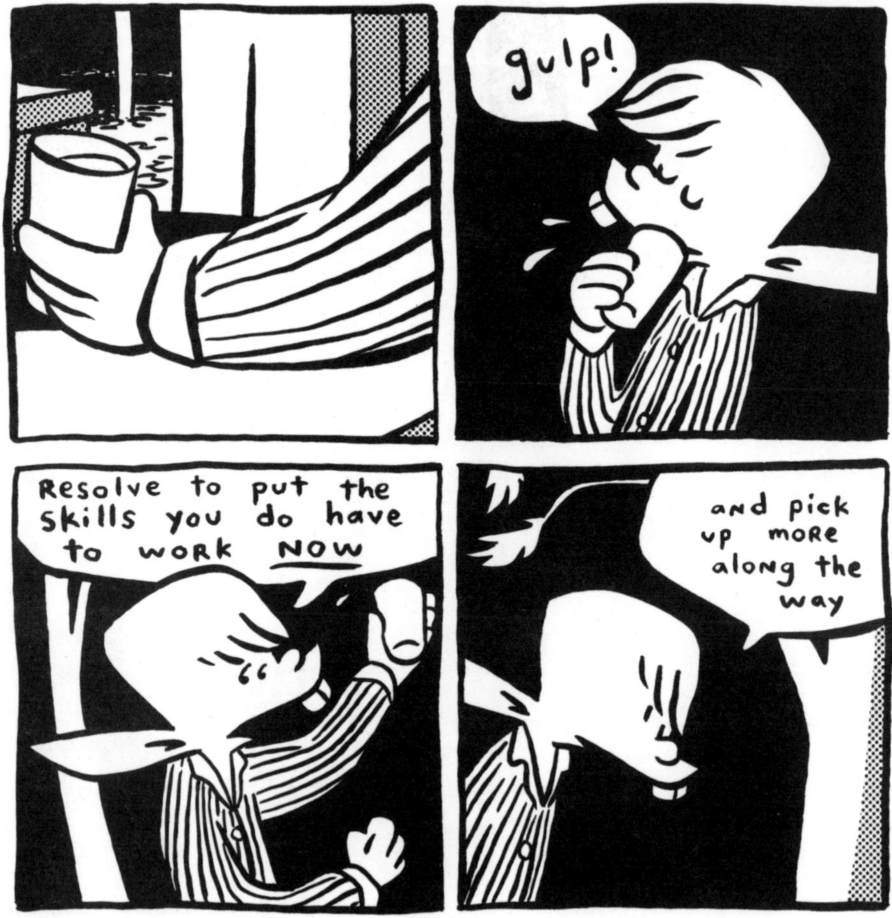
gulp!
Resolve to put the skills you do have to work NOW
and pick up more along the way

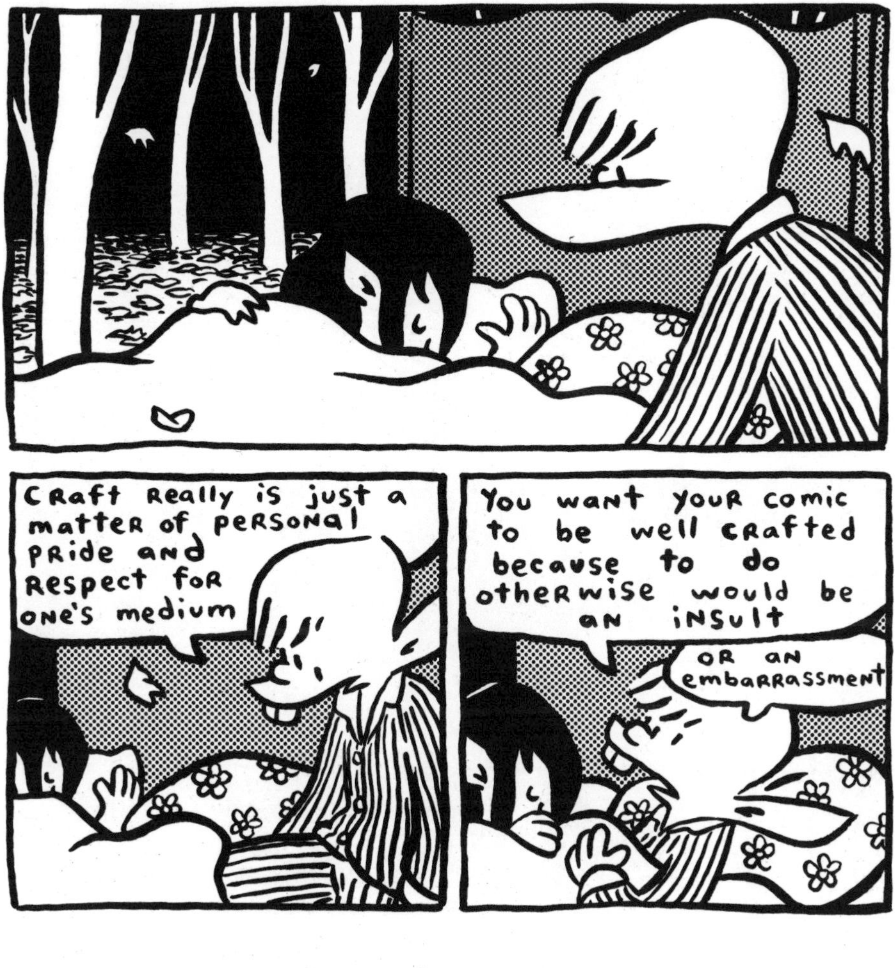
Craft really is just a matter of personal pride and respect for one's medium
You want your comic to be well crafted because to do otherwise would be an insult
or an embarrassment

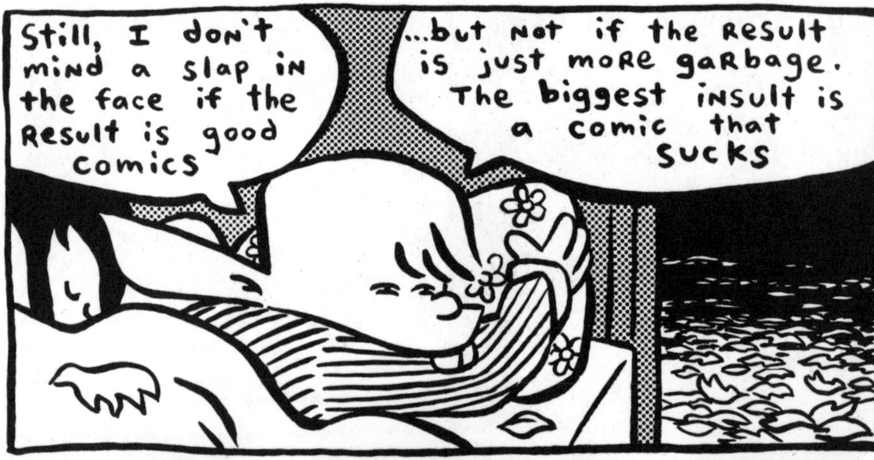
Still, I don't mind a slap in the face if the result is good comics
...but not if the result is just more garbage. The biggest insult is a comic that sucks
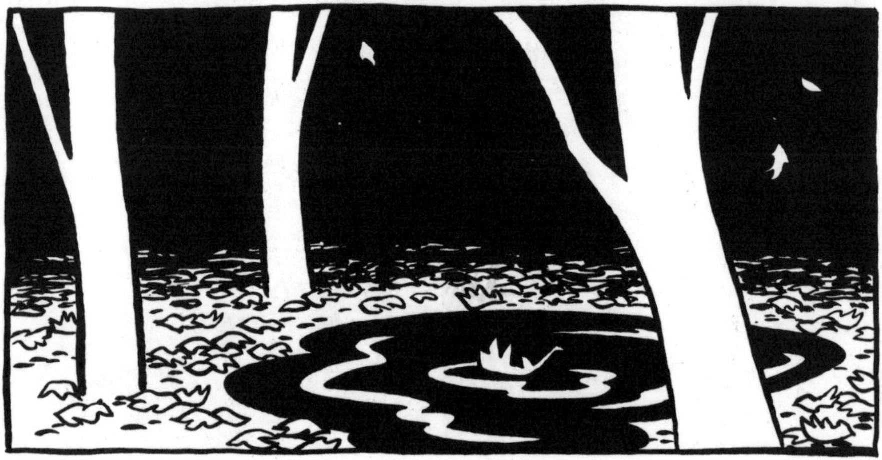

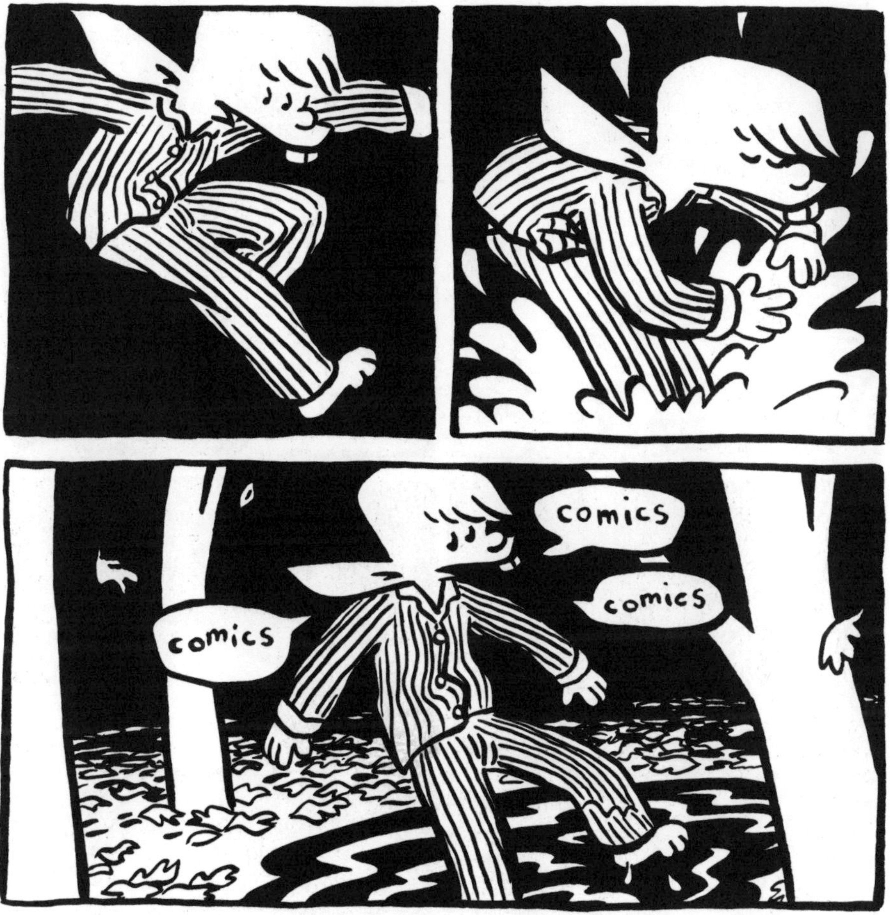
comics
comics
comics

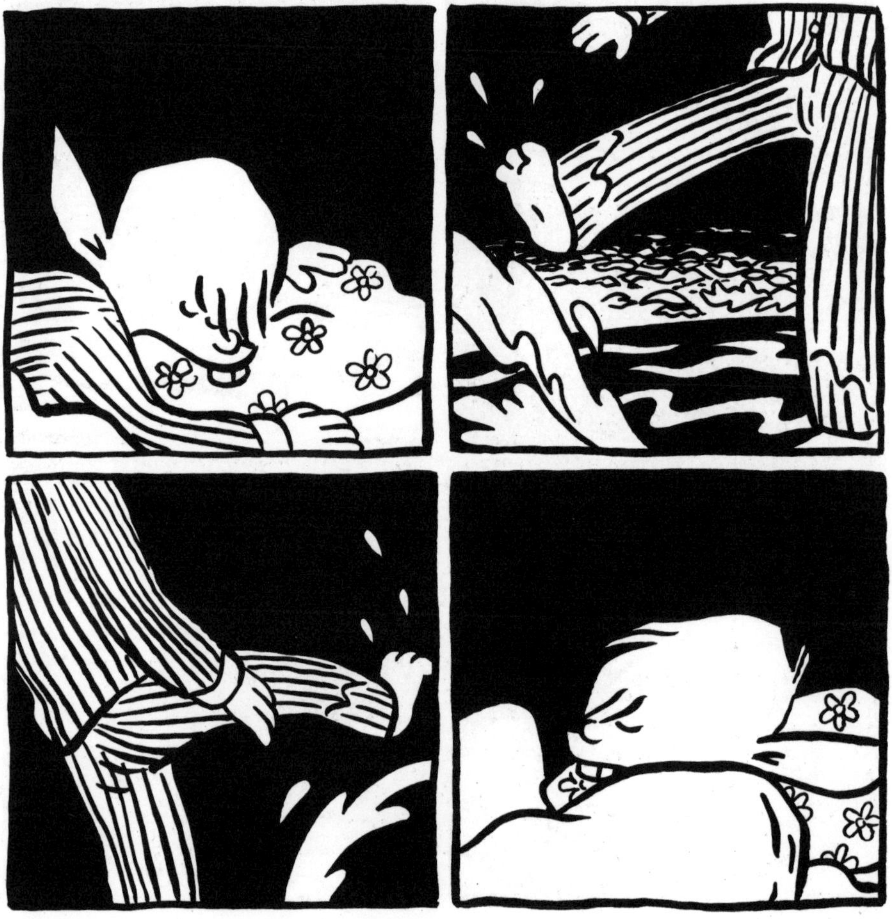

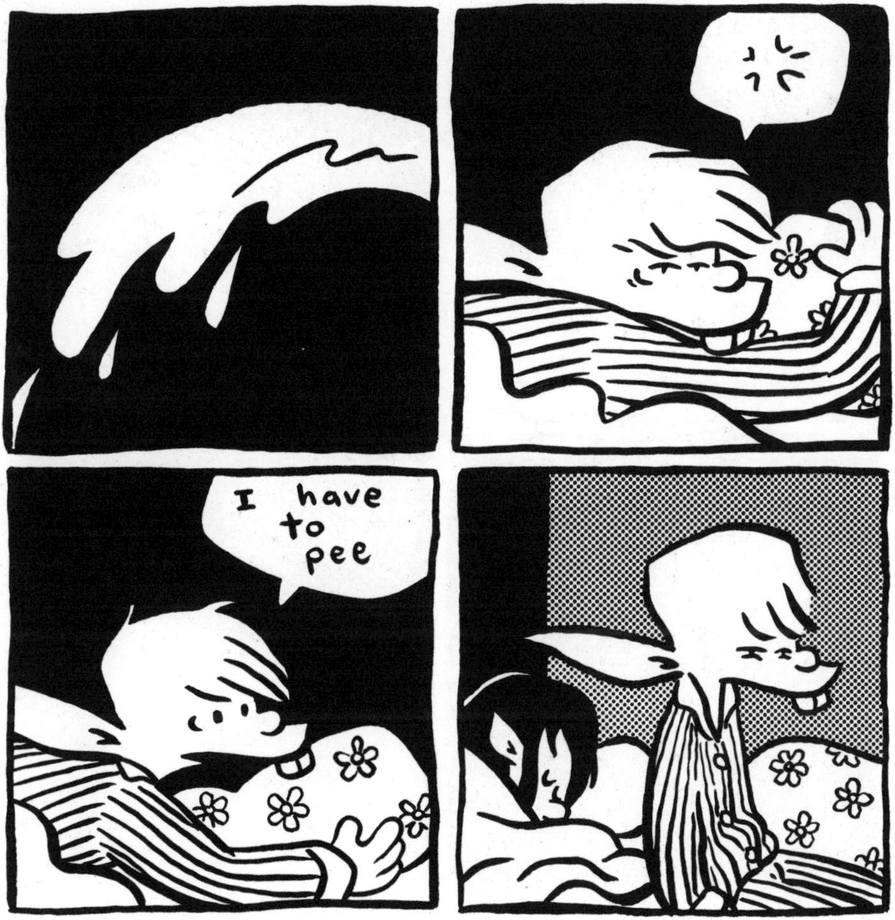
I have to pee

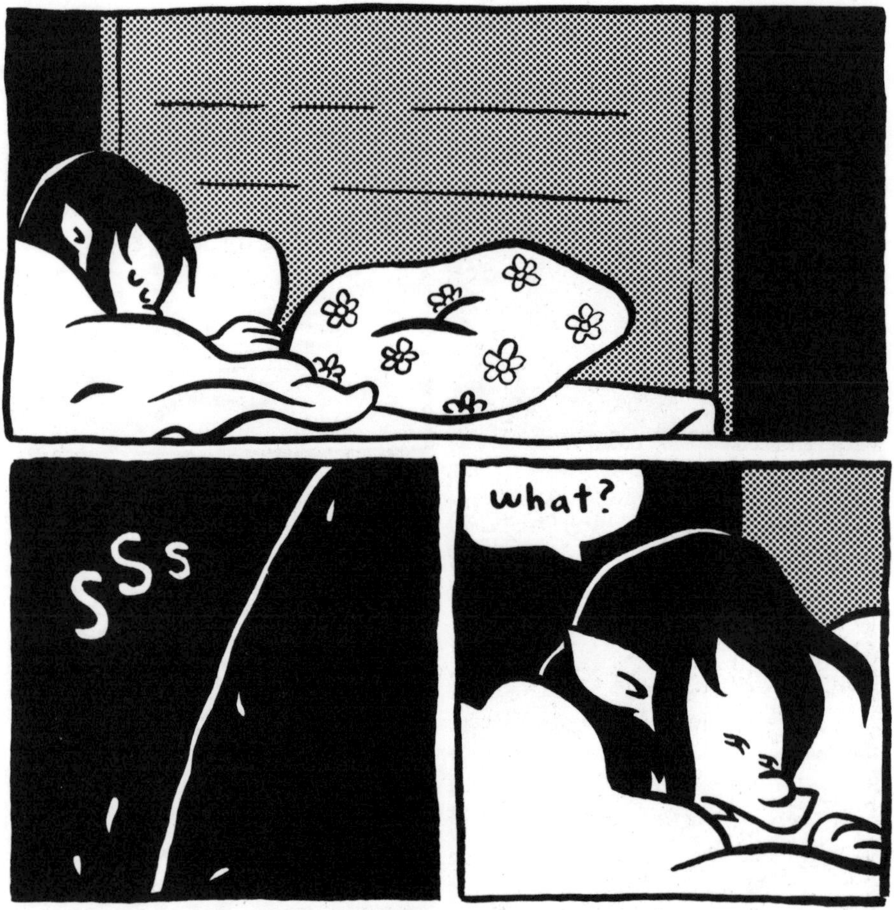
SSS
what?

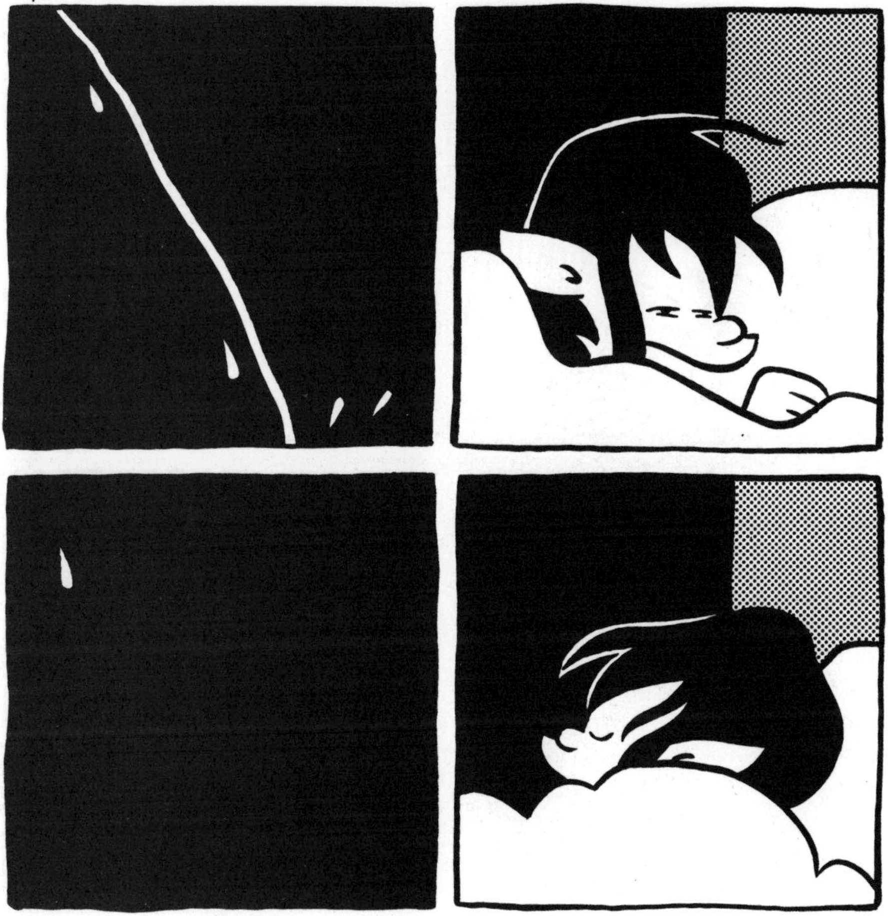

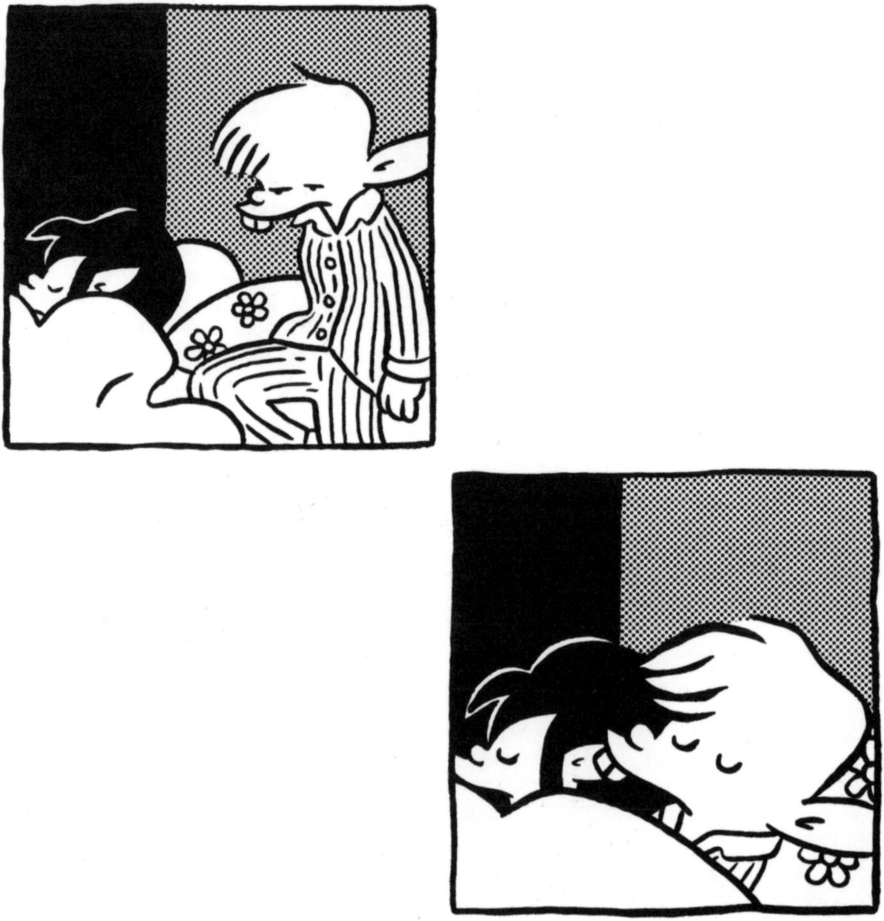

# SPELUNKING FOR SLIPPERY CAVE FISH

There have been many grand declarations made in this book. In the heat of an argument I can believe resolutely in absolutes, but then later, upon reflection, everything seems relative again. However, my arguments weren't really designed to convince you of what I believe is the truth, but rather as a tool to help me uncover the truth. It turns out there are many truths, and some of them are contradictory. In fact, these truths can be so contradictory that truth is not even the right word to describe them. Slippery Cave Fish is better. There are many slippery cave fish one can chase, and they lead us in different directions. You've got to shine a light and figure out what fish you're chasing, and what other fish are around you.

Otherwise, you're just spelunking blindly in the dark.